Book Cover Design by Dorian V. Esters

Published by: Divine Start Publishing

Printed in the United States of America
First Printing:
Library of Congress Card Catalogue Number: Pending
Greenwood, Anne
    Pearls & Pigs
ISBN-13: 978-0615481470

ISBN-10:   0615481477

DEDICATION

To my strong, intelligent, beautiful daughter; and my wise, courageous, handsome son. I found out that you were not the wind beneath my wings, you are my wings.

I also give tribute to my BFF (best friend forever), my prayer partner and confidant. You are a phenomenal sister both naturally and spiritually. I can't imagine life without you.

IN REMEMBRANCE

To my loving parents, I was blessed to have been appointed as your daughter. Thanks for pouring all you had into the formation of my life. What a heritage.

In memory of my loving brother, your life inspired me to live mine to the fullest. You will always remain close to my heart and with your voice whispering in my ear for me to "fan the flames".

ACKNOWLEDGEMENTS

With special thanks to 'Pastor Ruth', without your prayers and loving leadership this book may not have been written. I love you more than you know.

Thanks to Margaret Johnson-Hodge for generously giving of your time and sharing your expertise in book publishing.

Pearls

&

Pigs

The Backslider's Journey Home

ANNE GREENWOOD

DRG Publishing

Introduction

In this book, I have decided to compare the process of becoming the woman I was ordained to be, to that of the pearl, the "Queen of Gems". Pearls are lovely gems both naturally and spiritually. I have always admired the beautiful luster of a pearl. The pearl happens to be the only gem that is created from a living organism. When a foreign matter irritates the mantle (within the shell), the mantle secretes a form of nacre (mother of pearl), around the foreign matter's body and after several years, an encrustation forms the pearl.

The chances of cultured pearls being formed are very rare. If the oyster survives disease, climate changes, predators, typhoons and other killing agents, then a possible pearl can be formed.

My father was a handsome man, a strong shell. Working hard to maintain a beautiful home for his family, protecting us the best he knew how. My mother was very beautiful, fulfilling her place as the mantle within the shell. She was soft and nurturing, continually comforting us with love and wisdom. Being created by God they both housed the spirit of God, which stimulated the cultivation of my destiny.

In this story the Holy Spirit will actually represent the oyster found within the shell, slowly molding my life by releasing its anointed nacre all around me with his purpose of bringing me to a place of shalom, at peace, whole and lacking nothing. The influence of the Holy Spirit or of the oyster as presented in this book actually directed each phase of my spiritual growth. I believe God initiated it all when he placed my spirit in the DNA of my parents forming me before the foundations of this world, just as he has formed you.

I pray that the experiences I encountered within the various relationships and the faith walks I fearfully took, minister healing and restoration to every area of your life. The titles of each chapter express the thoughts and emotions of the grain or seed during its process of becoming a pearl. I have victoriously overcome some rough character building moments, just as the precious pearl evolved during its time of formation.

I sincerely pray that you choose to live the life of abundance that God intended for you to live. He loved us enough, that while we were yet sinners he died for us (read Rom 5:8); now it is our time to love him back.

Chapter 1

THE SHELL AND THE MANTLE
(A SHELTERED SETTING)

While growing up, somebody told me that when you save yourself for marriage and remain a virgin, that your husband would trust and completely respect you, treating you as a prized possession and esteeming you above all women. Boy, they were **wrong!!** Or should I say they forgot to tell me to read the small print attached to that presumed truth. The bible asks; who can find a virtuous woman? Her price is far above rubies (Proverbs 31:10).

I always knew this did not just refer to the physical aspect, and that the woman's character and mindset had to be virtuous too. So in preparing myself for marriage, I chose to study my mother's life. She was a very good role model for my sister and me. She taught me everything about keeping a clean home and making a peaceful haven for my husband to come home to. She showed me how to budget money and the importance of knowing your financial priorities. She also taught me how to cook and sew. I did pretty well with the sewing, the cooking has taken some years of practice, but I am quite good at it now. Whenever anyone would spend the night at our house, they would always talk about how peaceful it was and how well they rested while sleeping.

My parent's bedroom was like a sacred room. Mom

always kept it clean, crisp and serene. We had the liberty of going in the room to get something for her, or when I talked to her while she was making the bed or brushing her long, beautiful, wavy, hair. I liked taking a deep breath of the crisp fresh air as I stopped to enjoy the gentle spirit that filled her room. She once told my sister Deborah, that you should not allow any and everyone into your bedroom. It is the sanctuary of which your marriage is made and where it should stay. I do not think that Deborah and I captured the spiritual concept of that truth. Your relationship with the Lord must not allow invasion. He is a jealous God.

Mom never argued or disagreed with my dad in front of us, and that taught us to reverence and honor him. Deborah and I would be resting our happy little heads on our nice, clean pillowcases when she confronted him with any issues. I knew that she had discussed things with him because there were always changes made regarding something he said, or did. I would notice it within a few days. Sometimes I would see her kneeling beside her bed before going to sleep. It was a constant reminder for me to acknowledge God in all my ways. She wasn't a good wife because she was so pretty and loving. This responsible position was mastered by staying in constant prayer and asking God to help her be the helpmeet and mother He ordained her to be.

I received Christ as my personal savior at an early age, probably around 9 or 10 years old. I received the baptism of the Holy Ghost when I was 11. So God had an early start in my life, steering me in the way he would have me go. I was very obedient towards my parents and gave them much respect. I wanted to live long like the Word promises in Ephesians 6:1. One year during summer break, I did a course study through Moody Bible Institute. I wanted to learn the Word so that I could hide it in my heart. That was when I learned most of the bible verses I remember today. The Institute sent me a certificate of completion and my mom was so proud of me. Mom would let me have some of the younger kids in my neighborhood come over for an hour or so, along with their packed lunches, while I taught them about the Lord. We would meet in the basement the same time each day. I didn't know that God was preparing me for ministry. I was just having fun sharing Jesus with the younger kids.

After graduating from high school, my mom had me help her teach the neighborhood kids around the church on Friday nights. She was the junior church Pastor and used this strategy to increase the Jr. Church's assembly. Since they would not come to Sunday school, we had them after school. My mom already had the latch-key vision in the mid 70's. It was great helping my mom in this endeavor. I taught the youngest children and she taught the teenagers. The young people really loved my mom.

As I dreamed of marriage, I knew that I needed to marry someone that was saved or a believer like me. So I focused my attention on the young men that were saved. Or should I say, men that said they were saved. I was still learning how to discern the mind and purpose of people. I did not realize how much I needed to learn. I always let the young men know I loved the Lord and was only interested in someone that loved the Lord.

My dad did not claim to be saved but he was a dear heart. Even though he drank and got drunk at times, we still respected him as dad. He was a very kind and thoughtful man.

Whenever I talked to the boys, I was precise in stating that I wanted a sober-minded man, one that was drug free and did not drink or smoke. I tried to make this clear to all of them. There were no guessing games with me. The mothers at church always told us girls that a man would tell you anything to get you in bed. So I never believed anything a man promised me and always assumed his motives were wrong. The mothers had good intentions, but because of my lack of understanding, it may have ruined any chance for a decent young man to win my heart. I thought I was doing the right thing. I was convinced they were all liars, with the exception of the saved ones. I am sure I made things difficult for anyone who may have been interested in me. Most boys were shy around me just as I was around them.

Chapter 2

⌘

FOREIGN MATTER
(FINDING MY PLACE)

There was one particular young man named Adam that I liked in school. Adam was raised in a Christian home; he was well-mannered, full of integrity and musically talented. He was very attractive, generous, helped me with my homework, full of vision, very respectful and carried a fat wallet in his back pocket. I really didn't know how to handle such a man of valor. I was a bit shy and did not know how to express things to him as easily as he did to me. He had such a handsome smile, with his brilliant straight teeth. I could only wish my gapped teeth were just as nice; though I was the only one that seemed to have a problem with them. My sister and brother both had lovely straight teeth and I always felt less attractive because of my gap. I was so flattered when Adam gave me his ID bracelet to wear. He was all any sensible girl would want.

Well guess who wasn't very sensible back then? Not knowing that I was so insecure about my looks & intelligence, I subconsciously felt inferior to him. So I looked for something wrong with him. I didn't like a particular pair of pants he wore and did not know how to tell him. So I gave some off-the-hook reason to break up with him and our short-lived relationship was over. Just so you know, I was not anybody's fashion queen, nor did I know that name brand clothes even existed. Most of my wardrobe consisted of clothes that I made. I had no credentials for being anybody's fashion consultant. I gave Adam his bracelet back and *bam* it hit me, what in the world are you thinking? I was too embarrassed to try to explain and I walked away empty. It was obvious I did not know who I was, and I sure did not understand who he was. For some dumb reason I thought there were more where he came from. Besides, we were too young to actually fall in love and get married anyway; at least that is what I had been told. *If I only knew then what I know now.*

After many years, I finally realized I was a gem in the making, rising to an expected end. Adam may have known, and maybe he didn't, but life has taught me that such men of valor have what it takes to give proper homage to that of a virtuous woman, the woman I was longing to be.

Chapter 3

⌘

BEING AN IRRITANT
(WHO AM I?)

Although there were several boys that liked me
throughout my school days, I usually ended up with nobody.
The dating scene never happened. The church I was affiliated
with taught that it was a sin to go anywhere or do anything fun
like bowling, going to school dances or to the movies.
Coming to my house was a young man's only option unless he
wanted to take me to church or out to eat.

Thank God for today's revelation!!! Dating does not
have to be so boring and limited for Christians anymore. It did
not bother me though; it was just the way things were. I was
young and figured I had plenty of time to meet and date men.
Besides, it helped me keep my virginity. Temptation was
non-existent. Especially since kissing can make you have
babies… another piece of unclear advice I received. I thought
if I kissed a man more than twice, this switch would go off in
my head and I would be so out of control that I would have to
have sex. Maybe that can happen to some people, but not me. I
seriously do not believe it would be that easy if both your
hearts and mind were set to obey God's Word. I was serious
about staying pure for God and my chosen husband. This is not
to say that kissing or making out is appropriate when dating. It

is important to know your limits and stay within that safety zone.

My mom kept us very active in church. We went to all the conventions and youth congress meetings we could financially afford to attend. In so doing, I met many friends, both male and female. I learned to serve in almost every area of the junior church, including singing in the youth and adult choir. I assisted the Jr. Church deaconess by collecting and keeping record of all tithes and offering collected from the young people. I was trusted enough to handle the money of the youth. God gave me favor and I felt honored to be given such a responsibility. It is apparent that childhood opportunities sparked my interest in calculating money. Amazingly, my life career has been working in financial positions with such companies as savings and loans, banks, credit unions, annuity processing and reconciling mutual funds. God surely ordered my steps.

Though I socialized well at church and in the professional field, my social skills outside of these circles were null and void. I felt as if I was an irritant to the rest of the world. I was not cynical like most people; I was a true optimist believing in love and happily ever after. I felt like a misfit whenever I would discuss my dreams with most of my friends.

We were having a district meeting at our church one Friday evening and I met this very cute, but shy young man name Prince. He was there with his grandmother from out of town. We did not say much to each other. We were both very shy. One of the younger girls at church delivered messages back and forth between him and me. After church, we exchanged addresses and we began to write each other. Prince was so sweet. His letters were very endearing. Every now &

then he would give me a call. We could not wait until the next church function to see each other. At one particular convention, they showed a movie about the rapture. We sat through it together and watched very intensely. I had to leave before the altar call was made and he later told me he went up and gave himself to the Lord. I was so happy. He was such a kind heart; I could not believe he wasn't saved already. The letters became more frequent and I expected a call every week. Prince was tall and thin, with a smooth brown complexion. He had a warm friendly smile and was such a gentle man. He was a dreamer like me, thoughtful, understanding, protective, caring and now saved. We were both very shy and I cannot remember where we were when he gave me my first kiss. However, I remember he was trembling and I thought it was so sweet. I dreamed of being his wife and having his babies. I just knew we could be very happy together. He was the one.

Many of the young people at church thought we made a sweet couple. Even the older adults that attended Prince's church knew that we really cared about one another. His Pastor always teased him about me. Prince was crazy about me; at least that is what I was told. One day my sister Deborah and I were sitting on the porch, looked up and saw this young man riding his bike up our driveway. I couldn't believe it, it was Prince. He rode his bike over 50 miles to see me. I thought it was a joke, no way would anyone ride so far to see me, but sure enough, it was true. Deborah asked if he would like some water and he said yes please. I felt a little ashamed for not offering him first. He came well prepared too. He had his ID and his tire repair kit in his shirt pocket. Once I realized it was not a joke, I was definitely impressed. My mom and sister thought it was so Romantic. My dad thought it seemed very suspicious.

Prince was going to stay over night and I asked my dad if he could sleep in my brother's room. My dad thought I was crazy. If Prince was staying anywhere, it was going to be a motel. After we spent sometime together, I called around to find the least expensive motel in town. Prince did not have much money with him. He was allowed to leave his bicycle in our garage. Then my mom and I drove him downtown to the motel. Mom really did not like the idea any more than I did. However, daddy had spoken.

My dad was very protective of me. I was his oldest daughter and we had a good relationship. On Wednesdays when he was off work and fixing things around the house, I would sit and watch him repair radios, auto parts or things in the house. Sometimes he would give me a radio or two to work on. He saw that I found it very challenging. Once he gave me a little radio to fix. I do not remember what was wrong with it, but I fixed it! I was so proud of myself. Daddy was proud of me too. Only God knew how much I needed to learn all I did from him. I had plenty of time to use my mechanical skills later in life. He was not very talkative, a lot like my mom. They both had a great sense of humor though and we laughed a lot. However, things weren't very funny regarding Prince staying overnight.

I did not understand why Prince could not stay in our house. Prince was a very respectful person and would have been too afraid of losing me by trying something stupid right in my daddy's house. Prince said his stay was terrible; having no toilet paper was one of his complaints. I did not know that most of the bums (homeless) stayed at this particular motel downtown. I felt so bad for him. Nevertheless, he said it was okay for one night. Once word got to my Pastor about Prince riding his bike to see me, he said, "Now that's love". I was so excited to know someone could care about me so much. I never forgot Prince's display of affection, and I never will. We would see each other occasionally, and we wrote each other at least twice a week. Sometime after we graduated, he came to visit me again but he stopped by my friend Queen's house to show her what he had bought me.

Queen was a good friend and I always thought of her as my big sister. If we weren't singing or sewing something for a church function, we were sharing our dreams about the kind of man we hoped God would send us. We were always trying different hairstyles and asking one another's opinion about our attire; usually something, we had planned to wear to a church function. She was so creative; I just knew she was going to be famous for producing or designing something splendid in the fashion world.

After Prince left her house, he came over and gave me the sweetest little friendship ring. I thought it was so precious it really touched my soul. Prince was a good man. I really appreciated having him in my life. I kept the ring and wore it often, at least whenever my fingers were not swollen or too fat because of weight gain over the years. I kept it until someone stole it from me about 15 years later. Prince decided to join the army and asked if I would wait for his return. I was more than willing to. I missed him so much after he left and I wrote him everyday. He wrote me too, but the letters soon became far and in between. I didn't know why he eventually stopped writing. I asked a few times in my letters but he never would say. Eventually I stopped writing and our fairy tale romance ended. I did not understand what happened; I just knew I had to move on. It was apparent to me that he had a change of heart. He must have found someone else.

Chapter 4

⌘

SECRETIONS
(BEING PRIMED)

I was attending college and was taking a psychology class, which I attended on Saturday mornings. While I was waiting on my mom to pick me up, I stood outside of the indoor basketball court looking out of the main window for her to drive up. In came this man dribbling a basketball, he glanced over at me and said hello. I said hello and he continued his ball bouncing exercise as he walked into the gym. I just stood staring out the window thinking mom should be here any moment. Hearing the basketball dribble in the distance caused me to remember his presence. I pondered on the way he spoke to me. It was just a subtle hello. No lines, no stupid come on, just hello. I thought that was unusual, very different.

Then suddenly he was coming out of the gym talking about no one being there to play with. My first thought was, okay mom where are you. I was not afraid of him; I just didn't feel like being bothered. He simply walked over to me, start talking about no one being there to shoot ball with. I told him it must be too early for them. He jokingly said that maybe it was too cold for them to get out of bed. I remember being bundled up in my cute little black hat, scarf and black leather coat. It was early January and we were in Ohio, so you know it was cold. When I finally decided to look at him, he had such a handsome smile. He introduced himself as Tim and as I told him my name, my mom pulled up. I headed out to go home and he walked slightly behind me. Tim asked if he could have my number. I told him "if I see you again, I will give it to you then". He smiled and said, "Oh I will see you again". I thought yeah right don't hold your breath. I did not hang out at the university, so I really did not think I would see him again. Sometime that spring I was standing in the library at the university, all of a sudden, I looked up, and there he was, Tim was walking towards me. I thought wow, he is very handsome with his bow legged self. He smiled as he approached me and asked, "How are you?" I responded and we had a brief conversation. I told him it was good seeing him and started to walk away. He said, "Aren't you going to give me your number?" I told him I always try to keep my word, so I gave it to him.

Over the next few months, we spent a lot of time on the phone and at Pizza Hut. Tim came to church a few times and told me how he accepted the Lord as a young child. He shared with me how his uncle and aunt were missionaries over seas for a few years. He said he was saved and that he did not use drugs, smoke or drink alcohol. He was not from Ohio. He was born in the mid-west. Tim told me of his unhappy childhood, and how his dad abused his mother. He always tried to stop his dad from hurting her while his younger brother would hide and pray fearfully.

Since statistics show that most children raised in an abusive home tend to become abusive, I became a little concerned. He talked about how he would never hit a woman and how he could not understand why his mom stayed with his father. With this bit of insight, I decided to do a little research at the library to find out more about the subject of abuse. According to what I found and because of the person he appeared to be, I concluded Tim was one of the few who had learned to deal with disputes in a mature manner. Besides, he had the Lord in his life and that always overrides the devil's tactics. Well, at least I thought so. Anyway, I had found no reason to be suspicious of his anger or inability to manage it. Tim always treated me like a lady. Because of our work and class schedules, we couldn't see each other every day but we made sure we talked on the phone everyday. He respected the fact that I was a virgin and I appreciated his respect. I found myself in love with this man. He seemed to be the one I had been praying for, for a long time.

Then in early fall, something memorable occurred on my front porch. Tim told me he was thinking about joining the navy and wondered how I felt about it. I thought, here we go again. He explained that school and finances were not working out for him, and that joining the service was his best bet. He also told me that he loved me and wanted to marry me. He had no flowers, no knee bent and no ring for my finger. He never was good at planning things. The timing was right for him so he said it. The big 'm' word. I said, did you just ask me to marry you? He laughed and said yes. I paused in disbelief, seeming to drift off into another era or time. I quickly woke up and said yes. He reached out to hold and kiss me and I grabbed onto his strong smooth arms. I ran in the house to tell my mom. She was so happy for me. She knew how much we loved each other. I turned to him and said we have to get a ring. He said we would get one after he got back from boot camp. I was amazed, 9-10 months after meeting this man, and now we were talking about marriage. It was cool, I was planning a wedding, but not for anytime soon. Tim and I agreed to save up some money and take more time to develop our relationship. Once I received my engagement ring, we set the date. We would wait about 2 years to get married in 1979. I saw this as a great opportunity for me to focus on becoming that perfect wife. With him gone, I was guaranteed to be a virgin on my wedding night. I figured it was God's way of keeping us from getting it on prematurely. I would see Him every three to four months when he was on a two-week leave. There was talk of sending him to Guam for one year and he asked me what I thought. I told him I did not want him to go so he requested an honorable discharge and they gave it to him. Tim went back home and found a good job to provide for us.

Our day finally arrived and at last, we were married. The wedding went exactly as planned. Everyone was on time & the weather was beautiful. The bridesmaids wore a light baby blue & my maid of honor wore a pastel yellow. Tim wore white tails and the groomsmen all had on white tuxedos. We took loads of pictures at a local park and flower garden. Even the music was perfect. The food at the reception was catered and very delicious. All of my family and friends were there it was so perfect.

We spent the night in a local hotel and oh, what a night. Tim believed in foreplay and he loved on me for over an hour before he penetrated me. Lord yes, I was a blessed woman to have him as my husband and passionate lover.

After returning to my house to open and load up all the wedding gifts, we were off to live in the mid-west. The plan was for us both to work full time until he completed his final year in college. Then I would work part time and go back to college to continue my education. We were to return within a few years, to the east coast, probably Ohio. I could not imagine being away from my family for too long.

As soon as I met Tim's uncle, he hooked me up to the Christian radio station and invited us to his church. He took me on quickly as his special niece and was so kind to me. Tim & I had a very passionate sex life and I felt that saving myself for him was well rewarded.

The bible teaches us not to defraud one another (not to say no), because after marriage your body is no longer your own (1 Corinthians 7:3-5). So I never told him no, I did not believe in it, nor did I want to. Tim took me to see the first movie I ever seen as an adult. It was about Jesus, but I cannot remember what the title was. I was a little apprehensive at first; I kept waiting for something bad to happen. I was married now and no longer a member of the church I had been raised up in. I felt free to go see a movie with my husband. I had a great time. Tim was very patient with me when it came to things like that. He knew I needed time to adapt to doing new things.

Chapter 5

⌘

SIGHTLESS
(WHY IS IT SO DARK?)

After 6 months of wedded bliss, Tim started making excuses about going to church. Like needing to study and not wanting to miss a football game on TV. I started noticing inconsistent reasoning when he explained his whereabouts. I didn't know what was up until I came home from work one day. Tim worked second shift so he was always gone when I got home. I walked in our second bedroom to look for something and saw a joint, or blunt lying on the floor. I just began to cry. I thought no he didn't, no he didn't lie to me about using drugs. Did Tim lie about it all just so I would marry him? Why would anybody lie about something like this? Didn't he understand how important the truth was to me? How could he ruin my life like this? I didn't know what to do or who I could talk to. I was taught that whatever went on in your home, stayed in your home. I was facing something I did not know how to deal with and I began to be oppressed by the whole thing. This was my first experience in dealing with such a magnitude of anxiety. I called him at work and asked him about it. He blew me off. It allotted him more time to think about what he was going to say when he got home. Talk about a breach in contract! I felt betrayed. Had I saved myself all these years for a liar?   I wanted my mommy. I never thought I could become so broken over such a small thing. It really is true, "…it's the little foxes, that spoil the vines" (Song of Solomon 2:15). I never lied to him about anything; I knew how serious marriage was. Til death do you part. I never knew the blood vessels in my eyes could swell so large. I went into a pitiful state. I really cannot remember what he told me, but I do remember he denied it was his at first.

After time went by, the reality of Tim's drug use was prevalent and he was not going to quit. I was taught once married, always married. There was no way out for me. I had made my bed and had to lie in it. He would not smoke in front of me, but I could smell it from the kitchen late at night when I was in bed. I lost a lot of respect for Tim. He began to have serious mood swings. He found fault with everything I did, even with cleaning the apartment every week. Most men would die for a wife to keep house as I did. I was constantly annoyed by his unreasonable mood swings. He became inconsiderate, cruel and bitter towards me. Tim was no longer the man I thought he was.

Chapter 6

⌘

ENCRUSTATION
(SMOTHERED AND LAYERED WITH SCUM)

Then one day it happened. The unthinkable. One of Tim's cousins was over and we were sitting on the couch talking. Tim came home from the gym and asked about one of his magazines he had bought. I told him I had thrown it away. He was such a pack rat. We decided that after his magazines were over 3 months old I could throw them away. He swore he never said that. I swore he did. Next thing I knew he had his hand around my throat and was dragging me into our second bedroom, throwing me up into the back of the closet wall. He slapped me in the face, and then I heard his cousin yelling for him to let me go. When she saw me in the closet, she convinced him to let me go. He told me I had better replace that magazine or else. I was hysterical. I could not believe what just happened.

This was the beginning of the abuse, the abuse I thought wouldn't happen. I could not believe that this was the same man I married. The man that was usually very thoughtful and never failed to buy me a little something at the store on the way home from work or school, just because he loved me. On occasion, he would send my favorite yellow roses to me, just because. It was like living with Dr. Jekyll and Mr. Hyde. We would meet at the gym and he would help me work out.

He worked there part time so we had access to it all the time. He always tried to take me to meet people that were going places and doing things, people with vision. What happened to his?

His cousin said she had never seen him act like that and he must have gotten a hold of some bad weed. I thought all of it was bad, what did she mean? After the vicious storm calmed down, Tim apologized and told me I did not need to hang around his cousin. He did not like the lifestyle she was living. He had some nerve. I also knew this was his first step in getting me to isolate myself from every body; one of the things I had read about when I did my personal abuse study. This could not be happening.

I was over a thousand miles from home and I was not going to become his prisoner. It was obvious I married the wrong man. The only thing I knew to do was pray. I prayed for God to save him and heal him from his past and to give me the wisdom I needed to overcome this demon. The more I prayed the worse things got. The physical abuse would usually occur every three to four months or so. Each time he either choked me or slapped me. Some people have to deal with this on a daily basis.

Though I was not yet aware of the effects, the abuse had on me, slowly but surely I was turning into a person with low self-esteem. The unattractiveness I felt in high school resurfaced with the first slap he laid to my face. Tim did not think he was abusing me because no blood was ever shed and no bones were broken. I began to understand why some women stay in abusive relationships. There are various reasons, some not reasonable at all. I began to rationalize that he needed help, and I would be wrong to leave when he needed me. My other reason was to keep my wedding vows, "for better or for worse". I grew to despise those words. I was taught that if I divorced for any reason other than adultery, I would not be able to marry again until he died. I really felt trapped. My happy little world turned completely upside down. I started looking for women who might be interested in Tim. Then maybe they could entice him into an affair and I would be free to leave. I thought God needed my help on this one, there had to be a way out.

After his uncle found out what was going on, he tried talking to my husband. He told me if I needed him for anything to let him know. He was so kind to me, he treated me like his own daughter. My family did not know of the abuse. I could not tell them since there was nothing they could do. Well, I just did not want them to worry or know that I made a mistake in marrying Tim. I felt so much shame. It was overwhelming.

In March of 82', my mom happened to call after a sister from the church had stopped by to pray with me. I was so emotional from the prayer that mom could tell I had been crying. I told her about Tim abusing me just a few days before, but that I felt God was going to fix things for us. She said, "Well, your dad never laid a hand on me. If he does it again, you bring yourself home." I promised her I would. It was so great knowing I could go home and that my family still loved me. How could I even think they would not love me anymore? The seeds of the abuse had rooted well and the plant was beginning to sprout.

Chapter 7

⌘

THE HARDENING
(I AM SO AFRAID AND LONELY)

On April 11 of that same year my mother died. I was devastated. I became angry and cried out to God saying, "WHY DID YOU TAKE <u>MY</u> MOTHER? YOU KNOW I NEED HER." I felt abandoned and began to weep. Then the Lord said, "I AM your mother, I was your mother before she was, and will be til the end." I pondered, but I still didn't know why she had to die. My desire to be that woman God requires us to become, became a joke to me. I grew very angry with God. I know you are thinking how could I get angry with God? It's hard to explain, but I let him know how I felt. Only his merciful grace allowed me to go there with him. I now know that he understood my hurt and pain. He was right there with me and held me during my short time of mourning.

Tim was not capable of being a shoulder for me. It took me 10 years to completely mourn over the loss of my mother. He did not allow me to cry around him. Somehow, someway he began to ease up off me and act like somebody that had some sense. I thought my prayers must have been working. God does hear me. We began communicating again and I learned he was having difficulty with his reading. At that time, we did not know what it was, but we later discovered he was dyslexic. He was too embarrassed to tell me about his struggle. He had been in and out of college for almost 4 years. My plan to go back to school was still on hold. Even though he was still smoking weed, I had learned to just deal with it. Soon we began talking about having a baby. I felt as though I should wait until he received the Holy Ghost. He still was not going to church but he was making some positive changes. I was so excited about his restored behavior; I just knew we were back on track again.

Deborah, my sister, became engaged in 1983 and got married in early August. I got pregnant near the end of August. Tim and I were very happy. He was still being nice to me. I thought my prayers had finally been answered. We agreed that I would stay home and raise our baby. So after my maternity leave, I resigned from my job. We had a beautiful baby girl. I was so proud and happy to have her in my life. She was my little jewel. My aunt Celeste came from Ohio and helped me with my new baby. She brought so much comfort and peace to my spirit. She visited me in the hospital and gave me a manicure. I was blown away. How blessed I was to have my aunt take the time to serve me in such a way. I always knew she loved me, but that act really blessed my soul. I know it may seem like a small thing to some, but I felt like God sent an angel to minister to me. I felt very special, just like my mom always made me feel. Though she would not have been surprised, I know my mother would have been so thankful to her. There is nothing I could say to express my gratitude to Aunt Celeste. She was a great help and a joy to have in my home.

Deborah and her husband came to see the new baby about 3 weeks after she was born. Tim was uncomfortable with them being in our apartment. He always felt inferior to the man she married. They knew each other from back in the early college days. Deborah and her husband had gone to the store to get something and Tim and I got into a disagreement about the air condition being so cold. The next thing I knew he had me by my neck with my back pressed up against the kitchen sink. I just froze. I was recovering from having a c-section and I was not going to risk having a rupture by my making any quick moves. When he realized what he was doing, he let me go and he left. A few minutes later Deborah came in and found me in tears. They were leaving this day. She didn't want to leave me, so she began to cry too. I told her I was not going to go through this anymore and I promised her I would be all right.

Chapter 8

⌘

NACRE
(SOOTHING WRAPS)

Within a month, I was packed and headed towards home. As soon as my husband left for work, I packed my bags and got out of there. A few family members had gathered some money together and bought me a plane ticket. I was so happy, but still so embarrassed. I was going home to a motherless house, but my dad was there and he was glad to have me home.

I always loved my dad, but it bothered me when he drank. He was not a violent man, but the drinking made him turn into a different being. The spirit was very prevalent and his clumsiness and slurred speech was so belittling. It totally turned me off from any source of substance abuse. I always want to be in control of my actions. He would work all day and come home drunk sometimes. He was a business owner and a good provider for us all. He was what they call a functioning alcoholic. Once he was home he would fall asleep in his chair until morning or until my mom (when she was living), would make him go to bed.

My dad was willing to do whatever it took to take care of my baby and me. This was his first grandchild and he was so proud. He really was a good father in spite of his drinking problem. Of course, home was not the same without mom being there. I just could not rest in the house. I had been home two weeks and it just was not working out. My dad was so unhappy and lonely. We were not equipped to help each other. We both needed help.

By this time, Tim was calling me and begging me to come home. He swore he would go to counseling and get some help. He admitted he had a problem. Wow, it took me leaving for him to see it. Deborah and her husband let me stay with them a couple of weeks while I decided on what I was going to do. I went to see a minister and she told me my place was with my husband. She said that his problem was a sickness and that I promised to be with him in sickness and in health. Um, those wedding vows were back again. I did promise him and God. I decided to go back to Tim.

Chapter 9

⌘

THE AWAKENING
(THIS IS NOT MY DESTINY)

As soon as I got off the plane, Tim took the baby and walked away from me. I knew then that I should not have come back. I was trying to do the right thing, but the right thing was working against me. We took a trip to California to visit some of his family and boy was that a long ride. Tim was very agitated and just plain mean. Within a few days of returning home, we had another disagreement. This time I was feeding the baby and he threw a bottle of baby powder at me. It missed the baby's head just by a few centimeters. That was it. Forget what the minister told me. I had to get my baby out of this situation. We both needed out.

Sometime during this whole ordeal, I found myself stooped in a corner with all the lights out; pulling at my hair and trying to figure a way out. Then I heard the Lord say, "I can't use you crazy". That was it. I heard from heaven. God did not want me to suffer like this. I was free to move on. I was going to separate myself from this man. This time it was going to be for good.

Within a few weeks, I had arranged to move in with a friend. I promised her that Tim would not know where she lived or who she was. I did not want to bring any drama to her home. She was so sweet to my baby and me. Her home became my personal place of shelter. I will never forget her sacrifice and willingness to open her home to us. I understand the need for safe havens to abused women. Without them, family or friends, there is nowhere else to go. That is another reason why some women stay with their abusive partners.

It was then that Tim and I agreed to go for counseling even though we were living apart. We would meet at the counselor's office, driving our separate cars. My one on one session with the female counselor deemed very painful. She asked me questions that really cut me to answer. I acknowledged that the wounds were too deep and I could no longer live with this man. I began planning ways of getting Tim back. This was not the person I was raised to be; it was not I at all. I told my counselor that I could not raise my baby in a violent home. I had to stop this generational curse. I decided not to return back home with him and remained at my girlfriend's house. I planned to leave him without any help from my family this time. They had done enough already. I knew they did not understand why I retuned to Tim, but I had to know I tried everything.

After two or three weeks, a young couple from my church, named the Harts, invited me to come and stay with them. They had plenty of room, but most important, plenty of love. I stayed with them for at least three to four months. They were so kind and pleasant to live with. They were my heroes, in more ways then one. God definitely planned for me to meet them for such a time as this. They would never let me pay them for food or shelter. They insisted I save my money and not worry about owing them anything. God gave me such favor with them. The Harts proved to be loyal friends and have been a spiritual support for me throughout the years.

I was finally able to find a job and save up a little money to move out into my own place. The Lord blessed me with a nice apartment and Tim allowed me to have some of the furniture. He begged me to return to him but I told him it was over. My mind was made up. I told him if he did not harass me, I would not return to Ohio so that he could be close to his daughter. I also wanted my daughter to have the opportunity to see her grandparents and cousins from time to time. My plan was to save more money up and get a divorce. I realized I had to get used to the idea of being a single parent. Oh well, I wasn't the first and was not going to be the last. It was time to stop feeling sorry for myself and just focus on being a good mom. I have learned that people can only give you what they have. I was expecting Tim to be someone he was not equipped to be. He wanted to be my man of valor but he needed to be healed and delivered from his childhood issues. I was tainted now and needed deliverance and healing too. As bad as I wanted to, I could not help him while I was in a state of fractured emotions.

I used to sing all the time growing up and my alto voice was strong and smooth. One day I realized my song had left. I couldn't sing without crying. I lost the sound, the innocent praise and worship had been stained. I was living without a melody and life seemed motionless. I noticed that I stuttered when I talked and it was hard for me to look people straight in the eye when talking to them. The luster I once had was now scraped and tarnished. I did not know who I was or how I was going to continue. I just knew I could not stop; I had to keep moving forward, though I had no road map or personal tour guide to lead me on. I had a responsibility, a soul to teach, and a mouth to feed. I couldn't quit, I had to take care of my baby girl, my precious jewel.

For the 6 months that I stayed in the apartment, Tim never stopped calling early in the mornings or coming over and banging on my door. I told him if it did not stop, I would have to leave and go back to Ohio. He just would not stop harassing me. So I filed for a legal separation. The idea of filing for a divorce was too painful for me. I just couldn't handle the reality at that point. My expectations of marriage as I planned early in life only mirrored a happy bliss. Divorce never even shaded my mind. I really tried my best to save my marriage, but now it was time to save me.

Chapter 10

⌘

DAYS OF RECKONING
(I SOUND AND FEEL DIFFERENT)

I quit my job and moved back to Ohio to stay with my
brother Richard and his wife Doris. I spent all I had to move
back home so when I arrived in Ohio, all I had to my name was
one dime. Those first 4 months in Ohio were very trying. By
the judge's order in the legal separation, I had to leave my baby
with Tim for 3 months while I found a job and settled in. That
was the longest 3 months I ever experienced. I could not find a
job and I felt so alone. Once my baby was back with me, things
began to look up. She was two years old. We hung around at
home while Richard and Doris were at work. She played while
I sat worrying about finding a job. God used her to minister to
me while I sat in fear. Once she walked over to me, patted me
on my knee and said, "Praise Jesus Mommy, praise Jesus". I
was astonished. I just smiled and told her okay. Then I silently
began to praise the Lord. I felt a sense of peace come over me.
I knew God had spoken through her. Shortly after, one of my
cousins' told me they were hiring at a credit union, I applied
and I was hired.

The Lord blessed me with a nice job and I was able to
save enough money to buy a decent car. After a few months of
working I was unable to qualify for low income housing at the

price I was first quoted a few months previous. I had to find my own apartment. When I told Doris and Richard I needed more time to save up some more money they seemed to understand. But I soon found out Doris was upset about the whole thing. She became very moody and difficult to live with. After 2 weeks of dealing with her flipped personality, she told me she wanted me out. I explained to her that I knew I had been with them for almost a year, but I just needed a little more time to save up for a deposit. She didn't care, she wanted my daughter and I out. She said it was nothing I had done, she just wanted her space. I was crushed. Richard had no idea how she felt so I told him I had to move. He was furious, he said I didn't have to move until I was ready, but Doris was making it very uncomfortable for me. After we all came together to discuss the situation, I realized Doris was not budging on her decision. I asked if I could have 30 days to find a place & she grudgingly agreed. I called one of my cousins to borrow the deposit money and I moved out in 30 days just as I promised. I couldn't believe anyone would put a mother and child out like that. How could she be so insensitive?

I wrote to a friend (Victor) and asked that he pray for me. He was a kind minister I met when I lived out west. Since I knew little about the city, I was so afraid and I didn't know what kind of neighborhood I had moved into. My salary was not much to be desired, but I was still thankful for my job. I had to move where I could afford to live. I was short about $200 which was needed to meet the monthly budget. The child support I received was just enough to pay for our health insurance. I stopped to think how there were no financial worries while I was with Tim. He made a decent salary and we had excellent health insurance. I held my baby and began to cry, but held back the tears until she fell asleep.

I convinced myself, that nothing could be worse than living with Tim. If I had to struggle to raise my child, then that is what I had to do. Better to be poor and safe, than to be wealthy and live in such fear and abuse.

Victor responded with a phone call and encouraged me to keep trusting in God. I met him years ago and he was always nice to me. After talking to him, Victor told me that he and his wife had separated and would be getting a divorce. I was not aware that they were having any problems so this caught me by surprise. I really was disappointed and my faith in happy marriages was slowly decaying. He began to call me quite often and we established a nice relationship. He said he wanted to come and visit and I thought why not. It would be good seeing him again. He flew in to see me and stayed at a hotel near by.

It was so nice spending time with someone who could relate to what I was going through and who understood how I felt. He expressed to me how he always admired me and found me to be an attractive woman. Though I was flattered, I was caught off guard by his comment. Victor was very attractive and had a lot to offer. I told him I thought he was attractive too, but I would have never told him otherwise. My whole focus was on my marriage to Tim. I never looked at another man to desire him. At that time, Tim was the most handsome man I ever met. I really loved him.

Before Victor left, he gave me a few dollars to help me out. I didn't know what to think other than God must have been thinking about me. Our conversations continued and we began talking about seriously dating. Even though Victor was there to talk to, times were hard. I really hated the new lifestyle I was forced to live. I really wished I could just call my mommy.

As time went on, I noticed many single mothers getting all kinds of help from their boyfriends. Some of them weren't very attractive or virtuous, but they were being treated like queens.

Their babies wore the best of clothes and they were always getting their "hair did". I wanted to be treated like that; I knew I deserved it too. Once I realized they were having sex with these men, I did not know if I could do that. I was a virtuous woman; my price was far above all that. Yeah, right. Whom was I trying to fool? I felt like that virtuous woman stuff was all an overstatement. Doing it the old-fashioned way really did not work for me. I wanted my baby to have nice things and eat three healthy meals everyday too. She was not going to suffer because I chose the wrong daddy for her. It was on; I was going to be one of those fast girls. All you have to do is have sex and voila, all your needs are met. I told God I was turning my back on him. I literally did. When I told Victor I was giving up on God, he told me I could not do that. He tried to encourage me to hold on and everything would be all right. I felt helpless and did not want to hear it. I had made my decision. I did not want to be saved anymore.

The next time Victor came to visit, he tried to reconvert me. I told him to forget it. If I was going to hell, I was going good. I told him I wanted to start by having sex with him. I think I threw him for a loop, but not for long. He reminded me that he had a vasectomy years ago and I did not have to worry about getting pregnant. He gratefully submitted to my request with no hesitation.

Victor was not anything like Tim sexually, but he was good enough. He continually told me that backsliding was not the answer and I continually ignored him. He did not believe God saw what we did as a sin. I did not care to think what God thought. When he left I had money for my rent and later received a beautiful bouquet of flowers sent to me at my job, and I did not have to ask for any of it. This was cool; I found a way to make life easier. My baby was going to eat well this week. After Victor returned home, he called to tell me he really didn't have a vasectomy.

I instantly knew the possibility of being pregnant was great. You talking about feeling like a fool, I was fool with a capital F. I told Victor I was probably pregnant, but he didn't believe me. He came to see me again and the visit was not much of anything. I was not feeling him like before.

When I dropped him off at the airport, I did not know it would be the last time I would see him. Within a couple of weeks, it was a sure thing; I was pregnant and knew it was a boy. When I told Victor, he asked me to marry him. I said no. Since he lied about the vasectomy, I didn't trust him to be honest in a marriage. I just saw him as another liar. He said he wasn't going to take care of the baby and that I would be on my own. I couldn't believe it. He knocked me up and kept on steppin. I had heard of such things happening, but I would have never dreamed of it happening to me.

So much for me leaving God, I sure wanted to call on him now. I didn't though; I was too angry and full of rebellion. I had turned into a hurting, fearful, foolish, backslidden soul. You know the bible does say, "He who trusts in himself is a fool". (Prov 28:26, NIV)". It was a little too late for this scripture now. I thought things were bad before, I was on my way to finding out what bad really was.

During my pregnancy, God showed me the devil's

tactics that were used against me and how naive I was about the real world. I could not believe how much God talked to me. It seemed like I heard from him more then than ever. I was drawn by his love for me. I never experienced such a tender force of his love before. It is true; it is his loving-kindness that draws us. I soon found myself back in his presence, repenting and asking him to please forgive. Deborah and my cousin Rita were at the hospital with me during the birth of my son. It was great having them with me. My Aunt Celeste came and spoiled my son and me during our first week home. Loving and accepting him as much as she did my daughter. Victor sent me money while I was pregnant and child support up to 2 years after our son was born. Out of all my wrong doings, God was still merciful to me.

However, I felt rejected by the church folk, although they showed lots of love to both my babies. We church folk just had a problem with judging and pointing fingers. I remember one winter Sunday morning. I had neatly groomed and cleaned my children for church as usual they were just as cute as they could be. My daughter had on her little white patent leather shoes. Then someone made a smart remark about it being out of season for white shoes. Tears began to fill my eyes. I was so sensitive back then. They didn't see me, but I was holding back the tears. I had good taste in clothes too, I just wasn't able to buy them on a whim or whenever they needed them. I had to wait for God to provide in every area of our life. Those were the only dress shoes my little girl had. I felt like I would never fit in anywhere, the feeling of rejection grew consistently during those days. Although I fought it, patience became a part of life.

My financial struggles were even tighter now. I

remember my daughter opening the refrigerator door one day and saying, "Mommy we're poor". All we had was a gallon of water. I had $60 to buy food each month. That's right, $30 every 2 weeks, and from that I had to buy my toiletries, stockings and personal hygiene products too. I was blessed to have a sitter who usually fed them breakfast, lunch and dinner. She just didn't know how much it was needed. If it was not for the government program called WIC, we may have starved over the weekends. We ate a lot of hot dogs and fish sticks. I thank God for WIC: a government assistance program for women and infant children. Because of it, I never had to scrape to buy baby formula and food for my son. My sister helped either financially or by sending me hand-me-downs for my son. I know her prayers and constant support brought us through many of the storms. As far as the rest of the family, I didn't ask to borrow much from them, because I knew I might not be able to pay them back. I never asked for more than $20 at a time. I usually needed it to buy more food or gas to get to and from work. I knew everyone had their own family and bills to contend with. My son's Godfather was supportive too. Whenever I called for help, he would always come through.

My family blessed us several times during the years, but I realized my borrowing was on a long road to no end. So I decided to just bite the bullet and start trusting in God. Some people thought I was too proud to beg, but they just didn't understand. All my pride was gone, there comes a time when trusting God becomes your best source. Somehow, someway the Lord would get us through day by day. I know it was hard for most to understand my financial situation. We didn't have many single parents in my family and they could have never imagined the struggle. However, I was not going to be a baby about it either. "I made my bed, so I had to lay in it". Besides we all know, nothing is free. I learned if you keep asking for help, people will start giving you excuses about not being able to help you. Or they may manipulate you into feeling obligated into doing things they would not even do for themselves. Nor did I want them to think that I was taking advantage of them. That wasn't my way. Besides, where was the babies' daddy? It was not their responsibility, or their problem. I did the best I could with what I had. I stopped getting child support around the time my daughter turned four, just before her brother was born. Tim had lost his job and was not able to send me any child support. This went on for years. My daughter was 17 years old when Tim start paying child support again, and my son was 14 when his dad paid his. I felt like the world was on my shoulders. I learned to pray for my kids when they were sick, because I didn't always have the medicine they needed. I prayed for God to keep them healthy and they rarely got sick.

The Lord was faithful unto them regardless of my relationship with Him. I did not notice that God was using all of this to increase my faith. I just saw it as my only choice in caring for my babies. My son comforted me many times even though he was just a baby. Whenever I would hold him to burp him or just hug him, I would pat him on the back. He would always respond by patting my shoulder. It was as if God was using him to comfort me at times. When he started walking, he would always wait for me to walk in the door whenever we got home and then he would push the door shut after me, as if he was being my protective little man. It would always bring a tender smile to my face. God was showing his presence to me in so many ways, even through my beautiful children.

I longed for someone to ask me out, but no one did. I just

needed a break from the kids. Even though they were the sweetest babies any single mom could ever pray for, I would have loved to be taken to a movie or to a concert. I just didn't appeal to anyone. I guess I looked too needy or insecure. My friends started fixing me up on blind dates. I was in and out of relationships. Trying to find that hero, that friend, that real man. I didn't understand that "my maker was my husband and that the Lord of host is his name". (Read Isaiah 54:5)

I lived on the second floor of our apartment building, and had neighbors of all kind. One day I thought I smelled gas or something in the building so I called the gas company. The gas man could not find anything wrong with the gas line but he smelled something strange too. We eventually figured out it must have been a chemical used when doing drugs. Drug dealers had moved across the hall from me and were using their apartment to carry on their drug business. Later that summer, one of the neighbors in the next building got their car shot up. I heard the shots but did not know how close they were. My daughter wanted to go out and play, but her play days were over in that neighborhood. It just wasn't safe. After my kids were asleep, I would push my sleeper sofa up to the front door to deter anyone from coming in during the night. I did not want my babies to know how afraid I was.

When I first moved into the apartment, the Holy Ghost led me to anoint the front door. It was a thin hollow plywood door and the landlord didn't think it needed to be replaced. Anyone that wanted to get in would not have needed a key; it was that easy. Someone must have been praying for me. Maybe my dad and my sister. I didn't really feel threatened until the drug trafficking began in front of my apartment building. I never invited anyone over because I was so embarrassed about my neighborhood and apartment. We had roaches and I did not want anyone to know. I was constantly cleaning and shaking our clothes before we left the house. I probably saw one or two every few days or so. They weren't real bad, but I didn't want them in my home. Besides, I never had anything to offer to drink if anyone came to visit, so I conducted my social visits via the telephone.

Chapter 11

⌘

CHILLY WATERS
(I WANT TO GET OUT OF HERE)

I had a wonderful friend on my job, named Gloria. She was very endearing and a confidant. I could talk to her about anything. I told her about my struggles and she always kept me encouraged. It was as though God sent her to uphold me when I just wanted to give up. She shared my situation with her Pastor and brought him over to meet me one day. Sinister Ugh is what I will call him. They blessed me with some money, and it was right on time. The kids and I really needed some food. Sinister would call and check on me every now and then. I thought that was so nice of him.

Once he called very late at night. He said he was thinking about me and wanted me to know if I needed a shoulder to cry on he was always available. He said I should not feel bad about wanting to have sex again because it was natural. He said I could call him if I ever needed some. I was appalled. For one, he was another lying devil, ugly as all get out and married not divorced, not even separated, but married. I told him no thanks, I was not interested and that he was wrong in asking. I guess I didn't make my point clear. Within a week or two, he called again. I told him to come on over. He was there within a few minutes. When Sinister Ugh arrived, I had my bible spread open on the coffee table and I laid into him with the Word of God. He started stuttering and became so dumbfounded I wanted to laugh at him. I was too upset to laugh though. The devil thought he was going to trip me up with this joker. Sinister Ugh finally muttered, "I didn't know you knew so much about the Word". I told him that I knew enough to keep myself saved. Just because I made a mistake with the last man, did not mean he could be the next. I told him I knew I was wrong by having sex with my baby' daddy. Whom was he trying to fool? I rebuked him and told him to never call or come over again. That was the last I saw of him. I never told Gloria about it, but I found out later that he and his wife had gotten a divorce. Even though I had taken on a promiscuous spirit, I was still realistic in keeping a boundary. The bible says, "do not give that which is holy (the sacred thing) to the dogs (heathen)…" (Matt7:6a-Amplified). Whether you would call him a dog or not, he was undeniably permitting a doggish spirit to overtake him.

Then I met Maurice. A female acquaintance on my job introduced us. She thought he was a good and kind man. Maurice seemed considerate, honest and understanding. He was not quite my type. He was a bit on the chubby side. Nevertheless, I thought, maybe I should try another breed of man anyway. Maybe my type was the wrong type. Maurice owned his own home and had just gotten a divorce. He had five children and Lord have mercy, he was a minister too. We first chatted over the phone and he asked to meet me for lunch. He seemed to be such a gentle man. Not too long after we met, my birthday rolled around. Maurice wanted to do something special for me so he invited me over for dinner. When I arrived, the house was filled with warm candlelight. The soft candle light filled the living room and dining room with a sense of subtleness. It was so romantic, I was overwhelmed. He seated me & served my plate. We had Chinese food and it was good even though he did not cook it. He told me how special I was to him and I felt the tears beginning to fill up my lower eye ducts. I was glad he could not see what was happening. I didn't want him to know how much he touched me.

He was having some financial struggles since him and his wife separated, and I later found out his electricity had been cut off. He could have used all kinds of reasons to cancel our date, but he made the best of it. I was impressed. He had to file bankruptcy and ended up losing the house. We never went to church together because he believed in his home ministry. I soon learned this was another tactic the devil used on people to stop them from assembling themselves together. I began encouraging him to seek for new goals and to take better care of himself.

He lost a few pounds and became very confident with himself. We usually met for lunch and talked on the phone all night because he had a third shift job. I thought all he needed was for someone to love and help him get back on his feet. I couldn't believe how easy it was for me to have sex with him. My addiction, craving or enslavement of proving my love or devotion to a man just happened to include sexual involvement. It had been my plan for womanhood. Being a divorced woman never entered my thoughts or plot for adult life. I didn't know what to do with my healthy, vibrant, passionate nature. I never anticipated being alone.

I began to notice that many single Christian women in various churches were overweight but looking for a fit man. They relied on their addiction to food, which only gave temporary comfort to them. I believe I would have fallen under this addiction if I were ever able to buy that much food. In addition, there were those who were over their heads in debt because of their shopping addiction. I knew women that grabbed a pill whenever they had a slight headache or could not get to sleep. Then you have those that sat in their seat of self-righteousness with their hair did and name brand purses clutched to their sides hardly having any money in them. Some crept about in their private closets and masturbated with deep hurtful regret. I knew of a few that used good men and spoiled the chances of good women to have them. Others ran their mouths and became busy-bodies and of course, you had those that worked two or three jobs so they would not have to experience any time getting to know themselves and to proclaim, "I don't need a man, I take care of myself".

Well if the truth be told, nobody takes care of himself or herself, God is our provider. He has given us power to get wealth. My dear sisters, full of beauty and purpose, I know and understand your hunger for fulfillment. I recognize your cries. Though we mask our fears and failures in different ways, we all battle against the flesh, our minds. All of these are demonic attacks that some churches turn their heads to.

My weakness fell under the category of sexual sin. The church seemed to have this separate list of sins that seemed to be more tolerable than some of the others. I was a passionate lover and sex outside of marriage took an inordinate turn. According to "the church", it was more forbidden than many of the other sins mentioned above. I did not know that I needed someone to lay hands on me and bind the devil. I did not know I needed to denounce the enemy. I thought I could stop whenever I wanted to. I never felt like I needed a man to take care of me, part of being grown is taking care of yourself. Though I struggled, I was doing my best to make ends meet.

All the jobs I had dealt with handling cash or financial transactions and millions of dollars passed through my hands, but I was never tempted to steal or embezzle. I had issues, but stealing was not one of them. My mom taught me a lot about being a Godly woman and wife, but she also taught me to live independently.

I ain't even gonna lie though, I craved sex, I was a mother of two and in my early 30's. Being held by a man gave me great comfort. It was like a medicine, a soft cuddly teddy bear, a soothing wine. At this point, I felt trapped because I was in love with Maurice. I understood he needed me too. Though our needs were bona fide, neither one of us was capable of fulfilling those needs. We both needed some serious deliverance. Maurice thought I was exaggerating about my lack of funds and that I was trying to take advantage of him. Now how twisted was that? He loved going roller-skating once a week. I usually couldn't go with him because it was late at night and I could not afford a baby sitter. He never offered to pay for one either. One night I found someone to watch the kids for me and I went to the skating ring to surprise him. Well guess who got surprised? A few of his friends and I went out to eat afterwards and some other chick came too. He would not sit next to me at the table, but he sat with her. I was definitely being screwed. I ate, paid for my food and went home. I was in such denial. We argued later and without remedy, we broke up. Maurice was a minister, how could he also be a liar? I was confused, but he then came back asking for another chance. I agreed to give it another try. I wondered what kind of scent I was giving off. Only doggish creeps were trying to knock at my door. I was no longer innocent, but because I was always polite to people it was interpreted as being weak. I seriously loved people; it was what the bible convinced me at an early age to do. "Love thy neighbor as thyself". Perhaps I had forgotten how to love myself.

People were jealous of me on my job and I didn't understand why. Someone was always trying to discredit my work. I learned that you had to play games or office politics at work to get ahead. I was not skilled at all in this area. If they only knew the struggles I faced from day to day. I could not be two faced and brown nose people. Nevertheless, God always showed me favor and would get me pass it.

My home life was a constant challenge. My daughter had to be held back from 1st grade because she was diagnosed with dyslexia. I learned later that it was probably passed to her from her dad since it is hereditary. My daughter was suffering in her school studies and I could not help her. The only help available for her cost money, and we all know I didn't have that. When she was about 7 years old, she told me how she had been violated at the babysitters. She could only have been about 3 or 4 years old. I always felt like something was not right at the sitters, but I couldn't put a finger on it. So I had found someone else to watch her and my son. I did not actually know what was wrong until these 3 to 4 years later. I asked God why he hadn't protected her.

I was so angry, so hurt. God told me to praise him. I thought; you have to be kidding. Then I heard it again, "praise me". I began to praise him and then I heard Satan speak out. "No you ain't", he said, "no you ain't praising God". I was astonished. I confused the devil and he was blown away by my willingness to praise God in spite of the horrific news. This was my first experience in seeing the victory and overcoming the enemy through praise.

It was unbelievable how quick God moved in my spirit. He showed me how he did protect my daughter and that it could have been a whole lot worse. He let me know that by removing her out of the home actually saved her from more abuse. It was He that led me to find another sitter and that my son was only a year old and he wasn't harmed at all. I praised him the more and I realized in spite of all I had done, he still loved me very much. I knew if my mom were alive, my children would have been safe from all of this. She used to watch a couple of my older cousins' kids when they were babies. Everyone knew they could trust my mom. It was sad for me to think about the opportunity that she was missing to nurture her own grand babies. I really missed her.

My family did all they could to help. I have a dear cousin named Paula who took my little girl shopping for school clothes one year. I mean she bought her a big bag of clothes. I was so appreciative but I didn't know how to show it. She was a great blessing to us in those days, countless times. My family always made sure our Christmas's were good. I was thankful to be born into such a loving family. I have another dear friend named Brenda. I met her the year my daughter was born at one of Tim's family reunions. She lives in California and we hit it off from the very beginning, she really loved the Lord. We have kept in touch throughout the years and she was a great inspiration to me many times.

One Christmas in particular, Brenda knew the chances of my children having a nice holiday were slim. I was feeling a little low and depression was gaining fast on my heels. So one day I was sorting through my mail and noticed a letter from

Brenda. It was unusual because we rarely wrote one another. The telephone was our form of contact or communication. When I opened the letter, a $300 money order fell out. I was speechless. The tears began to stream down my cheeks. I exploded and thought, "There is a Santa Claus" and just began to laugh with complete relief. Brenda was a single mom too and it blessed me to receive such a gift from her. It was as if God was using different people at different times to bless my house.

I was never blessed from the same person more than twice, with the exception of the Harts and my family. I learned to lean on Jesus and not to expect things to work out the same way every time. I learned to trust God and expect him to come through for us His Word was my bond. In 2 Peter 3:9 it says, "The Lord is not slack concerning his promise as some men count slackness, but is longsuffering to us-ward, not willing that any should perish, but that all should come to repentance".

Mrs. Hart (Caren) would send me notes of encouragement from time to time. She would also dub tapes for me so that I could have some updated gospel music to listen to. She was such a thoughtful woman of God. I remember one Valentines, she sent the kids and I a box filled with valentine candy, heart balloons and confetti and perfume for me. I almost cried. She was the most loving friend I ever had. She knew I could never buy myself perfume and she tried her best to make sure I kept well stocked. That meant so much to me. Things like that kept my hope alive.

Chapter 12

୭

A NEW MATTER
(WHAT HAVE I BECOME?)

My income prohibited me from taking my kids to a decent day care. I could only afford home care. All my family had to work and no one was able to watch them for me. So I asked this woman from my church Mrs. Hurt, if she would be able to help me. We agreed on a particular dollar amount and she began taking care of them. I felt so at ease. My daughter took the school bus from her home and my son spent the day with her until I returned from work. Mrs. Hurt's husband was a minister and always asked how things were going. I always steered far from him and usually told him we were doing fine. Then one day my car wouldn't start so he picked me and the kids up, dropped them off at his house, and took me to work. He did this for a couple days, until I was able to get the car fixed. Mr. Hurt and I talked about the Lord and how the Lord would make a way for me. He told me he had been praying for God to bless me with a husband. I told him I was in agreement with that prayer. He said he had dreamed that my husband was walking towards me but he couldn't see his face. I told him I hoped the Lord would reveal it soon. A few weeks later, he told me he saw the man's face. I was very curious and excited about the new revelation. I asked him what he looked like. Mr. Hurt paused and obsessively told me that it was he. Oh my God, what in the world was the devil trying to do this time? I just started laughing at him. I told him that he had been led away by his own lust. I told him to cast down that thought. He was another unhappily married minister looking for a submissive woman. I was not the one. He never brought it up again. What was this? Was I destined to marry a minister? God forbid! Being a minister or Pastor's wife was not anything I would wish for anyone. I thought it was a curse, a hell on earth. However, ministers were drawn to me like bees drawn to the honeycomb. Maurice and I were still trying to restore our relationship. We were learning to be friends. Though we were both struggling in our finances, we really tried to keep one another encouraged.

It had been years since I had been able to buy anything new or up to date to wear. So people started giving me clothes to help me out and hopefully make me feel better. I really appreciated the clothes and wore them, but there is nothing like buying something on your own, something that suits your personality. My cousin Sheila shared some of her cologne with me and even bought me some of my own a few times. She blessed me to get my hair done occasionally and checked with me from time to time to see if we needed any food or milk. She was a continual blessing to our household. It definitely does take a village to raise a child. I was still sporting the once worn Gerri curl that I would turn into a blown-out dry setting every now and then. I really needed a makeover, but it wasn't my turn yet. My priority was taking care of my babies. Then it happened, I got a promotion. The first thing I did was to make a hair appointment. You would have thought I made plans to travel to Paris, I was so happy. Maurice was happy for me too.

He was in a bad financial state so I allowed him to move in with me for a couple of weeks until he was able to get his own place. He was helpful with buying some of the groceries though he didn't eat much. I was content to have him home with me. His kids would come over and spend the night sometimes. They were fun to have around. Maurice never raised his voice at me and he never showed any signs of a temper. He didn't smoke, drink or use drugs. I felt safe with him.

One day I called off work because I just wasn't feeling well. Maurice stayed around and pampered me. After a few days, I was still feeling about the same. When I kept falling asleep at my desk at work, I knew something was up. Duh, I thought to myself, you're pregnant! Sure enough, I was. When I told Maurice, he said he would not take care of the baby. I thought, HELL NO, not again. I was not going to bring another child into the world to suffer like the two I already had. I couldn't bear any more shame. Fear overtook my entire being and with little hesitation, I went straight to the abortion clinic. I let them put me to sleep so that they could take my baby. I didn't know if I would wake up or not. But God was merciful and he graced me to live on, healed from any physical complications that could arise. However, I was not free from the guilt and torment that festered within the deepest parts of my mind. I felt like a stranger in my own body. The purpose of my birth was tarnished. I had done the unbelievable. I had crossed the line. My morals had gone to pot. Though abortion is legal, I knew this was not of God. The bible says in 1Corinthians 10:23, "all things are lawful for me, but all things are not expedient". I actually fought against abortion in the past. It is true, the devil comes to kill, steal and destroy. He was truly after me and I had succumbed to his endeavors. I no longer knew who I was, or where I was going. I was definitely a frightened and lost soul. My relationship with Maurice ended for good. He was a hindrance and I considered him an accessory to the crime, he didn't even try to stop me from having the abortion. The only person that knew about it helped me keep it a secret from my family and friends for many years.

My daddy was a dreamer and he dreamed that somebody was pregnant. I told him it must be Deborah. Thank God she got pregnant shortly afterwards. I never lied to my dad before but I just couldn't tell him what I had done. He always kept in touch and I loved knowing he was there to talk to. However, since he lived out of town I did not call him much. He was diagnosed with cancer and barely lived long enough to see Deborah's baby boy born. In November of 91, he died. Daddy was the only man in my life I knew really loved me. I mourned for him, but knew he was in a better place. My brother Richard had prayed with him weeks before his death and he had repented and received Christ as his personal savior. Thank God, the prayers mom prayed for him was finally answered; and now daddy was in eternal peace.

I thought if I wanted a man in my life, I was going to have to settle for whatever. All the married women I knew or those involved with a man were unhappy. No one I knew had found Prince charming. I no longer believed good men existed. My love fantasy dream died. The expectations that I had of Godly men existing became a fairy tale to me. Survival was my new goal.

When I thought things could not get worse, I found out that Mrs. Hurt was abusing my son. One day when I picked him up I noticed he was holding his arm awkwardly. Mrs. Hurt did not know why. I took him to the doctor the next day and his elbow was dislocated. The doctor said someone might have shaken him. I was furious and tired of paying people to take care of my babies, but instead they mistreated them. They were good kids, but the devil was out to destroy them. I didn't know what to do, who to trust. I couldn't quit my job, we needed health insurance. Nevertheless, my God…had a plan. We were blessed to move into a brand new apartment complex with a washer and dryer included. I no longer had to wash our clothes in the bathtub or scrape for coins to use at the laundromat. I felt like I was moving into glory land.

Three weeks before we moved someone tried to break into our old apartment. It was on the weekend and my kids were with someone else. I was out and about running errands, I felt like I should stop home for a minute. The front door that God told me to anoint 4 years before had been tampered with. They had cut around the doorknob, but did not enter in. Nothing was missing. God had protected our home. He answered my prayers by keeping us safe from all hurt, harm and danger. God was so faithful to me. When we moved into our new apartment, I noticed there was a nice daycare down the street from us. They approved me for subsidized daycare fees. Now my son was happy and safe. My daughter was receiving tutoring in school and she was very responsible in carrying a key and letting herself in the apartment. I prayed all the time for their safety. I was never totally focused on my duties at work again. My heart was in the hands of other people. I really had a problem trusting people and my job performance was never the same.

Chapter 13

ஒ

CONSCIOUSNESS
(DEPTHS OF REALITY)

Black men never approached me on the job, at the grocery store or anywhere, the only men in town that ever took the risk and expressed their interest were older, drunk or high, with the exception of Sinister Ugh and Mr. Hurt. What did that mean? Did my forehead flash, welcome to all male dogs? I felt like I was invisible sometimes, as if I didn't exist. White men would compliment me and speak to me all the time. I was very confused about it all. What were they seeing? Did God have a covering over me? I could not figure out what the issue was then. I know now. Dead things attract flies, scavengers and worms, not to say that white men were any of these just because they approached me. I had become the walking dead. Though I was going to church, my relationship with God had been severed. I was not claiming to be a Christian, but I loved talking about the Lord. The purity and luster of my predestined life had become a stomping ground for the pigs in a pen. Pigs cannot recognize value, and they have no use for pearls in their slop. I began to understand the strategy the devil was using against me. The deadly language and lifestyle of the world became mine. Dishonesty, un-forgiveness, hurt, bitterness, insecurity, fear, hopelessness, suspicion, murder, defensiveness, anxiety, shame, nger, guilt, confusion and restlessness overtook my life. How did God expect us to live in such a horrific world? I found that I was no better than anyone else suffering and lost in sin was. Pointing the finger at all the deadbeat dads and doggish men was out of order. We were all victims, damaged goods bound by the enemy. God told me to stop calling men dogs, for they were his creation and he called them "good". The dog spirit may have been prevalent in their actions, but their true spirit was not doggish. Besides, I met some women who fell along the lines of being doggish, too. So I couldn't discriminate between the male and female gender. It was another evil spirit searching abroad for people of all kind that were vulnerable enough to submit to its deadly end. I had no peace, and was very lonely. My only drive, the only reason for living was for the sake of my children. As corrupted as I had become, I was still all they had. My friends at work always wondered why I didn't have a man. They thought I was the nicest person. I could never explain why. At the time I did not get it either. So I placed an ad in the personals and to my amazement, I had over 20 responses within the first day. I started going on blind dates. Everyone I met found me to be an attractive woman. It was fun. We always met at a public restaurant and I always got a free lunch. I saved a lot of money on lunch those few days. I decided to meet eight of the personals that responded, and they were some very interesting black men. Even though some of them were not interested in me, they could not believe I did not have a man of my own. Then I heard this voice on the other end of the phone; it was a friendly mellow tone, very engaging. I could not wait to meet him. Jerome is his name.

Jerome and I decided to meet during lunch, but he didn't have time to sit and eat. I worked downtown and he worked on the eastside of town. So I agreed to have him pick me up in front of the building where I worked. A good friend, I'll call Ashley, followed me down to the front of the building to take down his license plate number just in case I didn't return to work. Ashley was a very attractive white woman that was quite a few years younger than I was. She was a very loyal friend and really related to me being a single mom since a single mom raised her. She was such an encouragement to me so many times. She kept me laughing and always made me feel like I was the best single parent she knew. She has been a great inspiration to my children and me for many years.

When Jerome drove up, I was impressed with his slick black Maxima, well kept. When I started walking towards the car, I thought his eyes were going to pop out of his head. I opened the car door and he said, "Woo!" I asked if he was Jerome and he responded with "yes, yes". When I saw his tall dark stature, I realized this Negro is definitely from somebody's ghetto. I knew he would be the one to teach me the ropes, the players' game. After recognizing his voice, I proceeded to get into the car. I stepped my left leg in and was about to pull my right leg in when I felt his right hand wrapped around my left calf. I looked at him and said excuse me! He let go and said that he loved my legs and that I really didn't give myself any justice in the way that I described myself. Now mind you, I had on a long winter coat and a long peachy pink dress underneath. His focus was definitely on whatever he could see. I looked over at Ashley and she signaled that she had gotten the license number. I pointed to her and told Jerome that she would be calling the police if he didn't bring me back to work in time. He chuckled and said he would definitely have me back in time. As we drove off I took off my gloves and he thought I had the most beautiful hands. This man was trippin. You would have thought he never saw a beautiful woman before. He was certainly playing the player role. His look was hard, big reddish eyes, well dressed though. He had a nice low haircut and a million dollar smile. I had never dated anyone so dark before. He looked so rough to me, so street. I decided I wanted to spend some time with this one. I seriously doubted I would get attached to him. To say the least we were so different from one another. I knew if I wanted to do the dating thing, I had to learn to play the game. Jerome didn't know it, but I had just hired him to be the teacher.

After riding around for about 30 minutes, he said many of the women he had met in the personal ads lied about their appearance. I found that to be so stupid. Didn't the women think that he would eventually see them? Well, we decided to go out over the weekend to a movie or something. It took me all week to decide on what to wear. I did not have much of a selection, but I had a nice tight jean skirt that worked out fine. This was going to be my second real date within weeks of the last one. Not counting the many lunch dates I had days before. I took a deep breath a few hours before he picked me up. I did not know what to expect, but I knew that my player classes were about to begin. When he arrived, he looked very dapper. He had on a nice sporty shirt and some black dress slacks. We were off to get something to eat and to see a movie. We looked for something to eat, but there weren't many restaurants to choose from on my side of town. I thought he was just being cheap though. We stopped at Arby's and Jerome ordered a sandwich and I just got something to drink. I hadn't planned to eat because I was a bit nervous with this new venture. We left to catch the next movie and we had an hour to spare. So Jerome took me by a condominium he was supposed to have owned. He used some lame excuse about not showing me the inside of it because the occupant was still in the process of moving out. He even took the time to check the mailbox and played as if the junk mail that it possessed was his. I thought how stupid did he think I was? He suggested we go watch a movie at his place; he didn't want to go back and wait at the cinema any longer. This joker was a definite cheapskate and he actually thought I didn't notice it. Jerome was a skilled player. He pulled out a lot of tricks from his hat that night. I just could not figure out why he was trying to impress me with so much. Was he using someone else's car? Did he really have a good job with the government? What lie was he trying to cover up? He talked a lot of noise and I just played along with him.

Once we arrived at his apartment, I found it to be very cozy and quaint. I saw nothing that signified a woman living there. He didn't know that it made no sense to me for him to own a condominium and live in an apartment. Mr. Player was a little weak on covering his back. He offered me something to drink and we selected a movie to watch. I think it was on for about 5 minutes and his hands were all over me. I thought this man is crazy. Kissing and feeling on me like there was no tomorrow. He tried pulling up my skirt but it was too tight for him to budge. Who was playing whom at this point? I told him to back off and just chill. I had come to see a movie and that was all. Well guess who didn't get to see the whole movie. With 25 minutes left to the movie, Jerome thought it was best he get me home so he could get to bed. He said it was getting late. I messed up his little plan to seduce me. He found out quick that I had no interest in him. I was just there to see how the player simulated his game.

Chapter 14

ॐ

I CAN FEEL MY LUSTER
(I KNOW WHO I AM)

In the meanwhile, I had acquainted myself with a wonderful friend at my job. I will call her Deana. She had been raised in a Christian home and was living with her man and baby girl. We became very close and ate lunch together almost everyday. We called ourselves encouraging one another in our ungodly relationships. We even went as far as praying for one another during our 15-minute breaks. How twisted was that? I love her though, she is my girl. Although I was very concerned about her relationship, her man was a bit violent. Somehow, someway God showed mercy and allowed us to continue in our illusive ways. He even used us to minister to one another. I had the nerve to tell her she needed to get back in church and let God mend her life. She would reprove me as well and neither one of us could deny the truth. Even so, I continued to experiment with Jerome and the player's world.

Being a player was not as easy as I thought. The secret is not to care about anything or anyone. It is all about pleasing yourself. The opposite of what God says to do. The golden rule does not blend well with the way of the world. Most people are too afraid and bitter to "do unto others as you would have them do unto you". It just wasn't in me to deny my love for people. I didn't know how long I was going to be able to play with the player. Jerome was way out of my league.

We would call each other from time to time. He said he never met anyone like me before. He really didn't know how to come at me. Jerome was very consistent with his game playing. I had to call on my cousin Sheila, to help interpret some of his moves. Sheila knew how to play the game. She would explain to me every move he was making and what his next move would be. She honestly needs to write a book on how to play the player. Sheila became my personal player advisor. Thank God, her services were free.

Over a period of a few months, I began to admire Jerome's style and sexy body. He was about 6 feet, 190 pounds, and he was actually an intelligent man. We usually met at one another's apartment. He never attempted to take me out again. He probably could not take a chance in running into some of his other women. I found out that the Maxima was really his and he did have a good job working for the government. Then one day Jerome finally broke one of his player rules. He let me see him sweat. He always called before stopping by to see me. When he arrived on one occasion, he brought a peach flavored wine cooler with him. When I asked him what he was doing with it, he told me to drink some. I said "Jerome I don't drink and don't want any." I proceeded to sit on the couch and he walked over to me, reopened the bottle, put it up to my mouth and said, "Try it". I quickly turned away and gagged at the smell of it. He couldn't believe how much it repulsed me. I told him it stank and reminded him again that I didn't drink. He seemed surprised. He seemed lost on what to do next. Then he just asked, "Then how can I get you to relax?" I told him I was relaxed, I am always relaxed. I knew just where he was trying to go. I loved watching him try to conjure up a sexual proposition. I always made him come different by me with certain games he would play. Sheila always had me a step ahead of him. I tell you, she was my girl. She had been through some hard times too and we were struggling with our Jesus relationship. Sometime I did not think she knew what she was talking about, but she was always right.

Jerome looked kind of cute while fretting over what to do next. He was so uncomfortable and fidgety. I just smiled and asked, "Jerome, do you want some?" He gave a simple smile and with pleasure reached for my hand. I asked him, "Why didn't you just ask me? He didn't know why, but I did. It was not his style to ask. He didn't seem to care about being a gentleman when it came to asking. His style was to just let things lead up to it. He walked me over to the staircase and I led him to my bedroom. Lord have mercy, Jerome rocked my world. The last time I was done like that, was when I was married to Tim. Woo, help me somebody! Forget the game playing. I found my thrill, except Jerome was very withdrawn afterwards. He would not hold me, or allow me to touch him. He seemed incapable of opening up to any emotion. Maybe he couldn't believe I made the proposal before he did. Then again, he may have been dealing with something else. He may have been deeply hurting about something. I just began talking to him and he seemed a bit bamboozled. So I just started ministering to him. For real, I know you are thinking, of all places to give a word, but the words just started to flow from my lips. He just listened and slowly got up to leave. I asked if he was okay and he said "yeah". He never said if he enjoyed himself, but he didn't have to.

I had to share the news with someone. Of course, I called Sheila she had to know. We celebrated the occasion as some type of milestone won. She proclaimed me as player of the week. It was unreal, I actually played the player. Sheila and I calculated everything to the tee. After we said our good byes, I sat for a while and collected my thoughts. I actually started to feel guilty about playing with Jerome like that. I did not like it when it was done to me in past relationships, but he was out to play me too. I felt a little awkward about it but at the same time, it was great being the one in control. Our out of order relationship was on and I was determined to never be hurt by anyone ever again. My goal was to complete my "player course" with Jerome and equip myself with all the ammunition needed to withstand any future relationships. No one treasured the thought of having integrity or being honest anymore. So I laid aside those virtues when I was with him.

Jerome was a talker and we were on the phone regularly. He began to share some things about his childhood and his past relationships. Sometimes he would just come over to ask my opinion about this woman he swore was harassing him. Yeah right! Who was harassing whom? He talked about how she wouldn't leave him alone. But when he talked about her, you could tell he really loved this woman. I thought the nerve of him throwing her in my face. However, I was becoming his friend and he was beginning to trust my opinions. So I would just listen. It was part of the game; I wasn't supposed to have any feelings for him anyway. We never discussed being a couple; we just were whatever we were. Our relationship was purely sexual, or that's what I thought.

Then one day I found myself thinking about him and all the good talks we had. I began to understand why he chose to be a player. It was not something he inherited as male; it was a survival tactic. You know, get them before they get you. The very same reason I was using him to teach me the game.

I began to ask him for his opinion regarding some illusive man that was supposed to be interested in me on my job. Jerome didn't think my questions were cute at all. He showed his jealousy by talking noise like, "girl, you know you don't want anybody but me". I usually responded by saying, "but I'm only a booty call. I need a real relationship". The first time I told him that, he didn't know how to respond. After a short pause he replied, "Girl, you're not a booty call. You are different from anyone I have ever met. You know we got it going on". I would usually say something like, "oh yeah, how could I not know." Jerome had a way of saying things that just made me chuckle inside. Most times, I was amazed of how quickly he would come up with some of his off the hook lines. This ritual continued off and on for about one year. I would see or talk to him almost every day. Nevertheless, on holidays he would always disappear. I always spent them alone with my children or family. I started using his own player words on him and he never ever noticed. Probably because I used them with my own little twist.

Slowly but surely I began to fall in love with this man. After updating Sheila on what was going on one day, she declared he was in love with me. I did not want to tell her I loved him too, but she already knew. I had done an unacceptable thing. Players must never fall in love with the one they are playing. The game is over when that happens. I was scared now. What was I to do? Sheila said if I wanted to see how far it could go, just keep playing it cool. When he's ready, he will tell you how he feels. My ability to hide my jealousy was weakening and I hoped he would break soon. I had given up hope with Jerome. How long does it take a player to admit he's in love? Then one day we were lying in bed and he said he felt like something was wrong. He didn't know what it was, but within a couple days, his father died. He lived in another state and he had to travel home. It was a big shock to us both. He had a horrible relationship with his dad and now he was gone. I wanted to go to the funeral with him, but he wanted to go alone. He later spilled out that the other woman; you know the harasser went to the funeral with him. That was it; I was hurt that he would not want me to be with him at a time like that. He had shared so much with me concerning his dad. I decided to start backing off. I had gathered enough player information anyway and it was time to move on. I stopped calling as much and gave him some excuse about not being able to see him from time to time. My final synopsis was that lying and cheating only begets lying and cheating.

I guess he thought my retreat was part of a game tactic and his calls came more often. I would only talk to him occasionally and see him once or twice within a 2-week period. One day, we were at a recreation center near my apartment. My children wanted to play on the swings and stuff. After I played with them a while, Jerome and I decided to sit on the ground and talk while the kids continued to play. As we played in the dirt with some sticks, we exchanged just a few words. Then there was a prolonged silence. Jerome looked up from writing in the dirt and said, "I think I am in love with you". I didn't know what to do or say. I just looked at him and his eyes were filled with so much sincerity. He said he knew he had a lot of issues but he really enjoyed being with me and that I had taught him so much. I was bewildered. I taught him so much?

Taught him what? I still couldn't form any words. I was dumbfounded. Then he just looked at me to respond. I asked him what in the world did I teach you? He said, "How to be a friend". Well I was messed up for real now. We kissed, hugged, and got up to play with the kids. My heart was pounding so fast, I just wanted to lie down and pretend I was floating on one of the sailing clouds going by. Sheila was right again. She honestly should be paid for her player knowledge.

Jerome's life was really messed up though. He was still seeing Miss Harasser and trying to keep me from knowing. But I was through with that part of the game. I finally figured out that she was now living with him. He was so pitiful. His appearance became sloppy and he started slipping on some of his lies. It seemed as though he was falling apart, but of course, he dared not be honest with me. That woman was running him ragged.

He called me one day to let me know she had moved out. I asked him, "When did she move in?" He realized he had never told me. He asked me to come over so he could explain. At this point, it didn't matter what he said, but I heard the sincerity in his voice and I knew he wanted to be straight up with me. So I went over to his place. After I listened to his explanations, he walked me to my car and said that he was glad Miss Harasser was gone. I sat in my car about to leave his apartment parking lot and I told him that it was time to quit playing with himself. I told him that God loved him and was going to take everything from him if He had to, just to get his attention. I told him to go to church and find God. He looked at me and did not know what to say. He finally said, "will do, you are probably right."

Our relationship did not change much after that. I knew I

couldn't trust him enough to make a commitment. However, I still loved him.

Chapter 15

&

THE VOYAGE
(JOURNEY OF RELEASE)

My prayer life was being restored and I began hearing from the Lord more often, especially in my dreams. The channel of communication was open to him more than before. In the fall of 1993, God led me to start praying for my husband. Yes, husband. I was hesitant at first because I never prayed for someone I'd never seen or met before, but I felt led to pray as if I knew him. I prayed for his health and wealth, the weather he faced, and any of the problems he had to overcome. I prayed for him to be loosed from any bondage or stronghold. I began to prepare myself physically and spiritually because I believed my husband was soon to come and that he was going to need whatever I had. All this was an act of faith. I told no one because this was odd to me. I knew it would only give folk something else to joke about concerning me. While praying for him, I could actually feel him receiving it. It was as though I could feel God moving. I knew God was talking to me, finally, I knew his voice again. On December 5 or 6th, God gave me a dream that altered my way of thinking in regards to time and purpose.

I saw myself on a river standing on a small raft with a small white sail or flag attached to the pole. It was as if I surrendered to something. I was leaving town and it seemed like no one cared. There were family members standing around the seashore, but I could only remember my sister and brother. They were walking away on the bay while my raft was drifting off. I thought fine, don't miss me too much, and forget you too! I couldn't understand why they weren't seeing that I made it off all right. The least they could do was say goodbye. As I stood on this raft, I realized I was all alone. I couldn't remember if my children were with me. It was a lonely moment, but as I looked down beside me, there was a dead man lying on the raft and suddenly the raft began to sink. Before I could react, I was coming up out of the water on a nice size motorboat. It was zooming full speed ahead and the dead man was gone. I didn't know where I was headed, but as the boat went under a bridge, the river became a street and I was standing there with my children. The cars that were parked on the street looked to be of the 1960's and 70's. People were just walking peaceably up this street. My children and I began walking when I noticed they didn't have their book bags or maybe it was their coats. So I told them we had to go back and get them. We turned around, walked up to this house, and opened the door. My Aunt Celeste, was there walking around looking for her husband, my dad was sitting over to my right at a small table in the corner tearing down on some fried chicken. I walked to the back of the house, which seemed very small. I began looking for the kids' things. While walking back to the front of the house, my friend, Rod, was walking out of the bathroom with only a towel wrapped around his waist. His head and body were dripping wet from the shower he had just taken. He smiled at me as I spoke in passing. I then walked over to a table that was next to the front door. Rod came behind me and hugged me, trying to get me wet. I just acted as if I didn't want to be bothered, so I bent over to look under the table. I saw three Easter baskets wrapped in clear yellow paper. I knew it was a surprise for the kids and me so I just acted as if I didn't see them. My dad kept asking, "Who made this chicken" and I finally told him that I did. Aunt Celeste kept smiling and walking around looking for her husband. With Rod still attached to my waist, we both began to laugh as he tried to get me wet. I looked back over my left shoulder to say something and Jerome walked by. He had just come in the house and saw Rod with his arms around me. He gave me a look that could kill, but he kept walking. I felt in the dream it was time to release him out of my life. Then I woke up.

God told me that the Easter baskets symbolized the season he was going to manifest one of his promises. So he told me to walk in praise and look forward to the season of Easter in 1994. He kept telling me he was taking me out of the old & into the new. Well sure enough, early Easter morning, Jerome called. He said that he was in the neighborhood and had been drinking and didn't think he should drive all the way home in his condition. He asked if he could come over and sleep downstairs on the floor until the morning. I told him we were all sleep and did not want him to wake the kids. He promised he would stay downstairs and leave in the morning. I unlocked the door so he could let himself in; I went back to bed. I heard him open and shut his car door and I went to look out the window to make sure it was he, it was. As soon as I lay back on the bed, I heard him coming up the stairs. I got up and met him at my bedroom door. I softly spoke so as not to wake the kids. "Jerome, I told you to stay downstairs." He said, but where's my hug and kiss? I closed the door behind him so the kids would not be disturbed. I gave him his usual hug, kiss, and turned to walk towards my bedroom door to point his way out. I told him, "Now go back downstairs". He started pulling off his shirt and had his pants half way down his legs before I could say, Jerome! He grabbed me and said again, "Where is my hug?" I was still trying to be quiet; I softly responded and said, "I gave it to you already, now get downstairs."

In the three years of knowing him, I had never seen him like this before. It was too late for me to think about the big mistake I made by letting him in. I grabbed his shirt and told him to put his pants back on. He grudgingly grabbed his pants off the floor and started towards the door. I asked him to put his pants back on before opening the door and he asked if I would go downstairs with him if he put them back on. I told him yes. I did not want him to open the door with just his underwear on in case one of my children had awakened. Well, all he heard me say was yes and he grabbed to open the door. I put my hand up to stop the door from opening and he turned and looked at me with such rage. Just like the look, he gave me in the dream. The next thing I know I was flying across my bedroom. I did not stumble or slide, I flew. Jerome had lifted his elbow up & shoved me in the chest. He hit me so hard; I had a bruise on my chest for 3 months afterwards. I had flash backs from the abuse, I suffered with Tim. The only thing that stopped my fast flight was the wall. When I came to myself, I must have felt like the prodigal son (Luke 15:17), looking up out of the pigpen, wondering what in hell just happened? Jerome was still standing by the door waiting for me to react. I just sat there and said a quick prayer. Jesus, my God, what do I do now? What was Jerome going to do? Again, I thought about the children.

Jerome asked me if I was coming and I said yeah. So I let him open the door with his clothes in hand and quickly followed him out and down the stairs. Even with all the noise, thank God, the kids were still asleep. He lay on the floor and I laid on the couch. He would not leave and would not stop talking about lying with me until I got on the floor with him. I was thinking; just give this fool what he wants. So I did, it was horrible. I was silently crying and he was smiling and acting as if he never had it so good. Our relationship came to an excruciating halt. Again, the bible says, "…and do not throw your pearls before hogs, lest they trample upon them with their feet and turn and tear you in pieces." (Matt 7:6b Amplified).

I thought God definitely used this incident to sicken me about ever having sex with him again. I actually thought he knocked the sexual devil out of me. Morning had arrived and I had gotten Jerome up and ready to go. The kids were up ready to enjoy some Easter candy. Jerome kept apologizing and I told him not to ever call or come over again. He said he didn't know what got into him. He felt like fighting somebody that whole night he was at the club. I didn't care what the reason was; I told him he had no excuse to hit me. He agreed and went his way.

I was so thankful nothing else happened. God knew he had to take care of me. "Surely grace and mercy followed me." I did not know what I had gotten myself into. What a rude awakening. The enemy, the pig (the unclean spirit) that I was battling with, was not the male species, it was Satan himself. "For our struggle is not against flesh and blood, but against the rulers, against the authorities, against the powers of this dark world and against the spiritual forces of evil in the heavenly realms" (Eph 6:12, NIV).

I quickly repented and began my journey back into the fold of the good shepherd. My mind was made up for sure. I wanted to be whole again, I was tired of trying to take care of myself, doing things my way. There is without a doubt "no place like home." God said, "...if my people, who are called by my name, will humble themselves and pray and seek my face and turn from their wicked ways, then will I hear from heaven and will forgive their sin and will heal their land" (2 Chron 7:14 NIV).

My search was seriously on for a good Pastor. I needed someone with a "today word." I did not want to be patted or just added to the member roll. I wanted all that God had planned for me. Everything that was ordained for my life. I wanted to be me again. The bible says, "We all like sheep have gone astray, but now you have returned to the shepherd and overseer of your souls" (1 Peter 2:25, AMP). Weeks had passed and Jerome was trying to turn his life around by going to church. He called and asked if he could talk to me. He really felt bad about what he had done. I agreed to see him and just like all the others, he begged me to take him back. I couldn't, I knew I shouldn't, so I didn't. I was not going to allow another abusive relationship in my life. I needed Jesus and would accept nothing less.

I began visiting a church that had a wonderful praise and worship service. God's presence ministered to me and opened me up to his voice again. The Pastor was wonderful in bringing forth the Word, but the congregation was too large for me. I needed a smaller church, one that would be able to minister to me one on one. I wanted to be whole. The Lord was really talking to me and letting me know how much he loved me and showed me how he protected my children and me over the years. He showed me how he wanted to rid me of all the religious traditions and that I too, had a judgmental spirit. I didn't want to believe that one. I hated the way church people always talked as though they were better than others because they didn't commit certain sins. I was not as bad as most, but I had enough in me to be rid of.

After all I had been through; I couldn't point a finger at anyone. I understand how sin can entrap your mind, your emotions and your life. If the devil is your daddy, you are capable of doing any and everything. Because of anger, fear and disillusion of the truth, people can get addicted to drugs, food, sexual spirits of all kind, money, obsessive behavior, alcohol, egotism, the list goes on. They are devices the devil uses to pacify, or create a false sense of protection, power and love. I had nothing but compassion for the lost ones. I could actually relate to why the hurting hurt. I needed a Pastor that would not be judgmental. Someone that was compassionate and powerful enough to help me get delivered. Someone that I could trust not to make sexual propositions towards me.

Then I learned that a couple that used to attend one of the churches I belonged to had started a bible study. I never went to any of the bible studies, but after a year or so they started a church. I really had a lot of respect for these people and I planned to visit their service one day. But they were having services on Saturday and I found it very difficult to adjust Saturday church services to my weekend schedule. That was my sleep in day. Though I knew I could trust this minister because he truly loved God and his lovely wife.

One Saturday I finally got up and went to the church service. The praise and worship was awesome. I felt like God's presence was all over the place. The Pastor preached about ridding our lives of the traditions of men and those of the church. Family reconciliation was the focus of this ministry. This was the language I had been hearing in the spirit since I decided to turn back to God. Then the Lord moved on the Pastor and he called for anyone to come up for prayer. I found myself going up. He looked at me and said he felt a fleshly spirit on me. It blew my mind. This man of God saw just where I was. I could not hide and he was not going to pamper me either. He wanted me to be free, as badly as I wanted to be. I thought, this is my Pastor, this is my home. I began to confess my sins and he prayed for me like no other Pastor had before. When I went back to my seat, I couldn't believe I confessed in front of all these people. But I felt no shame and they showed no sign of being judgmental either. I felt nothing but love. I just cried and I could feel some of the hurt in me minimizing. God's Word says, "If you seek me, you shall find me" (Matt 7:7). I found it to be true, I was so relieved. No one knew how much I felt like I had just stepped out of a wilderness. As the service was about to end, I was sitting on my seat and the Lord said, "I will never leave you or forsake you" (Heb 13:5). I thought, I know that Lord, you have proved that to me time and time again. Little did I know why he reminded me of such. Only he knew what was to come and he knew he had to reassure me of his purpose and plan for me in my new church home.

Every time I stepped foot in church I would cry

uncontrollably. I had held back the tears for so long I never knew I could cry again. The anointing was so strong in the services. I didn't know the Lord was releasing and cleansing me from some of the spiritual debris I had picked up during my backsliding years. I stopped wearing any eye makeup to church because I would end up looking like a raccoon by the end of the service. I didn't know how much God was moving in my life, but I knew something was happening. Hope was being restored and I actually felt like I could be totally delivered there. I was very comfortable because I was not judged by what I had to wear. My children did not have many "church clothes" to wear but it didn't matter. We were finally accepted as we were. Thank God, the Pastor and his wife were more concerned about our souls.

Chapter 16

ૐ

THE EXTRACTION
(NEW BEGINNINGS)

After about 3 months of attending the new church, it was requested that the church be in prayer for Pastor because he was diagnosed with colon cancer. We were believing God for a miracle, I knew I was. My faith had been restored and I knew God would do it. I was praying for my Pastor and waiting on God to heal him. Then one day I received a call. I was told my Pastor had died I didn't know what to think, I didn't know how to feel. He was supposed to be healed; he was the Pastor I searched for, what in the world happened? I just wept, I loved him so. What was his family going to do? What was going to happen to the church? So many things went through my mind. I just could not believe it until I saw him asleep at the funeral. I felt at peace, because I could see that he was at peace. Then I heard the Lord say again; "I will never leave you nor forsake you." It all made sense now. I understood why the Lord spoke this to me when I first came to church. He knew I would feel forsaken again, just like I did when my mom died. By speaking this to my spirit, I was comforted.

Though I suffered with symptoms of desertion, the seed of abandonment never took hold. I didn't know what to do. Did I have to seek another Pastor? Could there be another shepherd for me? I just felt led to sit tight, so I did. For about six months or so, we had a temporary Pastor, who served until the church knew what the Lord wanted us to do next.

Ultimately, the late Pastor's wife agreed to take the position and my soul was relieved. Many people had already left the congregation because of Pastor Jacob's death. Now others were leaving because they did not believe a woman should be a Pastor. I knew better. It's not the type of vessel God uses; it is all about the spirit that dwells in it. I grew up around many women Pastors and God blessed their ministries too. Pastor (Ruth) Jacob, was strong and continued to be just as faithful to the ministry as before.

I watched her as she presented her first sermons. She seemed very shy, but very sincere. She would never look up at us while she delivered the message, but little by little, that shy spirit died. As she grew in the position of Pastor, I was growing too. She taught us to be consistent and persistent and to be faithful unto God and to the ministry. She taught us to pay our tithes and offering and to give sacrificially. When I moved into my first apartment the struggle was so great, the faith I needed to pay my tithes was thrown out the window. Even being under the leadership of Pastor Ruth, I struggled with paying my tithes on a consistent basis. As far as giving, Pastor Ruth taught me through a personal experience of how to give sacrificially.

I was having one of my bad money days and I thought to call her. I asked if I could borrow $100 so that I could pay a bill. She sort of chuckled and explained that she didn't have the $100 but she would give me half of what she had. I just began to cry silently. I was lost for words. I was not sad or upset, I felt blessed. She was so willing to take from her needs, her household to help me. She gave me $15 and I felt like it was ten times more. Her faith stunned me. I wanted to be able to give like that. To have the faith I forgot I once had in my youth.

The Lord always had the church praying and fasting about something. I had never fasted so much in my life. I thought the traditional fast of one day a week was good enough. It seemed as though my crying during church service would never cease. I had so much weeping to do. The loss of my parents, the death of my marriage, the struggle with inferiority, the abuse of my children, the torturing fears, the years of degradation, the horrid abortion, the promiscuous lifestyle, the pain of hopelessness, the financial suffering, the loneliness and most importantly the loss of time with my Lord and Savior. I did not realize how much I was holding in. I always made jokes about my situation, it was easier that way. I could not face the reality of it all, without laughter, it was just too much.

Then one day during service, the tears didn't come. I was able to make it through the entire service and maintain a dry face. Now I could start wearing my makeup to church again. I did not know what was going on at the time but God had purged me from so much. I noticed that I was looking at people eye to eye again. My confidence was being restored, the old me was coming back. I felt like I was important, as if I had a reason for living. My sense of humor was being restored to its original place. Even my children seemed different too.

Our praise and worship team consisted of high school seniors, which dissolved after they graduated and pursued their various fortunes. Pastor Ruth prayed about the situation, then asked me to do the praise and worship. I knew my voice was not up to par, but I thought I would fill in until someone else could. I didn't have a problem with being a servant in any position of the church. Besides, it couldn't have been hard to do. I was used to leading devotional service years before and I thought it would be similar in presentation.

Well, I found that it was nothing like leading devotions. The spiritual attack that encompasses you is unbelievable. I was on a revelational path of no return. I remember the first few times I stood before the congregation. I thought the organist could play whatever I sang. Octavia is an awesome musician. So I just started singing some of the songs we had been singing along with some old devotionals. I could not believe how much my voice cracked and how I would run out of breath so quickly. I was seriously out of shape. My singing skills had been diminished and tainted by the trials of life.

I began to pray consistently and seriously about my new appointment. I did not want to be a hindrance to the service or to the deliverance of anyone in the congregation. The more I prayed the more the devil attacked me. There were a few times I stood before the congregation attempting to lead praise and worship and I literally felt something choking me and closing up my throat. I began doubting my ability to do praise and worship. Fear of inadequacy and failure began to haunt me every Friday night before Saturday's service. However, I pushed forward in prayer, got up every Saturday, and did it anyway.

I didn't know why Pastor Ruth would get up and leave the pulpit while I was going forth at times, but I later found out that she would go and pray for my breakthrough. The devil was out to stop me. He knew my victory was in my willingness to lead the praise at all cost. I realized how much he hated me. Within a few months, my notes were not cracking anymore and

I was able to sing longer without running out of breath so quickly. With all the fasting and sweating while dispersing all I had in praise, I lost a few pounds here and there. I began to understand the fault was not entirely mine, but the enemy was doing all he could to stop me from giving God the glory. He knew that praise was my strength, my victory, and his defeat. Thank God, the Pastor and the congregation endured with patience regarding my endeavor. They always encouraged me in some way or another.

Now, let me take your minds back to the Easter season and the dream that I had. Please recall my friend Rod that had just taken a shower and was trying to get me wet. He suffers from sickle cell and has had problems with his spleen because of it. It just so happened he had his spleen removed during this Easter season. God refreshed his body by way of surgery. When I visited him in the hospital, he said he did not have to deal with that pain any longer. I was amazed how this incident also proved the dream to be from God.

Subsequently on May 2, I received a phone call. It was Prince; yes the same dear Prince from my teenage years. He had relocated himself, the week of Easter and had been trying to get in touch with me ever since he moved to town. He told me how he walked from one city to this and how God blessed him to get three rides along the way. I was so excited to hear from him, he was always so precious to me. He met with the kids and me at a local park and we talked about old times. He was still that gentle man I remember him being. He explained how he just left everything and moved here. He said it was time to let things go. He wanted a better life for himself. We talked over the phone again and I had him over for dinner. As we were standing in my kitchen talking, I heard the Lord say,

"This is your husband." I was speechless, how could this be? Was God being for real? I had heard this before, way back in our younger day when our church was going on a bus ride to some church function. Prince and I were sitting together, hand in hand. As I laid my head on Prince's shoulder to fall asleep, I heard the Lord say, "This is your husband." I never told Prince, I never told anyone.

As I reminisced our sweet yesterdays, I didn't want to accept it now. We were two different people now and besides, I thought, "God, he's not even saved." The spirit of the Lord quickly replied and asked me, "Who says?" Wow, God put me in check. I was way out of order for judging Prince. Only God knew his heart.

I couldn't tell Prince what was just revealed to me; hopefully he wouldn't be concerned about being more than a dear friend to me. As I looked toward his heart, God showed me a vision. Right in the midst of Prince's chest, God revealed a portrait of Prince. He was clothed in a robe and wore a crown. I heard the Lord say he is a Prince. Prince was talking while all this was going on and I had to interrupt him. I told him that God just showed me that he was a Prince. I could not convince him that I was serious and that I had never experienced anything like this before. He just shrugged his shoulders and thought I was trippin. I knew I wasn't crazy. What God had showed me was as real as I was standing there. My sister and brother disagreed with me being with Prince. He just wasn't good enough for me in their eyes. I had to learn to be careful of what to tell people when it came to this spiritual experience. If God does not reveal or speak to anyone else about certain things, they will not receive it or believe it. Some things must be kept to yourself. Just like Abraham when he took his son Isaac to sacrifice him. He didn't announce it in the town flyer; he just kept it to himself and obeyed God.

The dream made more and more sense as time went on. I was on a journey and I had to go alone. The part about my dad eating chicken in the dream left me wondering. He liked fried chicken but he never ate it as he did in that dream, but guess who does? Prince loved fried chicken so much that he seemed to suck the air out of the chicken bone after devouring the flesh. No exaggeration, do not mess with him when he is eating his fried chicken.

One day Prince decided to tell me his main reason for moving to my city; he said he told God he was coming to get his wife, to find me and marry me. My mouth dropped open & I stood with my eyes bucked in disbelief. Reluctantly, I began to tell him how God told me he was my husband years ago and again since we reunited. He was so elated! I was numb.

I realized how badly wounded he was and that God wanted to use me to show His love. I told the Lord I needed to be loved, He said as I showed love to Prince, I would be loved. Fear began to rise and I asked God to help me. "Please give me the wisdom to love him the right way." He revealed some of his past to me. When God showed me he had battled with alcohol and drugs, I didn't understand why he wanted me to marry Prince. Why me God? Why do I have to go through this? Why isn't he delivered already? I had my own issues. The Holy Spirit reminded me that I prayed for God's will regarding my mate. After all the other relationships I had endured outside of God's will, it was time for me to trust him in this one. In preparation for getting married, I tried to find ways to prolong the arrival of our wedding day.

Yet another confirmation came. My sister Deborah had a

dream over 10 years before. She dreamed about a man and me being separated and enduring different trials of life to reunite later. For years, I would ask Deborah if the men I dated could have been the one in her dream. She would usually say no and sometimes she didn't know what dream I was talking about. Then one day to our amazement, she was over visiting with her family and Prince was there too. Deborah said, "...when Prince passed by I just realized he's the one in the dream, it was him all along." I asked her, "What dream?" I had finally forgotten all about it. Now wasn't that something. I couldn't believe God confirmed it through someone that doubted me just a few weeks before. From that moment on, she knew I had heard from God, she believed Prince and I were in the will of God.

I was still dealing with the fact that Prince was to be my husband. I decided to place a fleece before the Lord, like Gideon did in the Bible. I misplaced a picture that was taken of Prince and me on graduation day. I had not been able to find it for a couple of years now, but I knew it was in the apartment somewhere. So I told the Lord that I would marry Prince if I found the picture. I planned that I would marry him within a month of the picture being found. Of course, my intention was not to find it, so I did not look for it. I figured I would buy some time and drag it on as long as I could. I told Prince about my petition and he didn't say much of anything. But within a day or two, Prince had a dream. He said he saw the picture in between some papers in a box stacked underneath another box. I forgot Prince had the gift of dreams. There was only one place I had boxes of paper on a shelf stored, so we went together to look and sure enough it was stuck in between some old bills. I was speechless, Prince just smiled and asked, so when is our wedding date? He wanted a wedding; I just wanted to get married. I already had a wedding; I did not need another in this lifetime. He insisted, because he didn't have a wedding the first time he was married. I prolonged it, stretching the date an extra month, so we married 2 months later.

Chapter 17

ళ

THE POLISHING
(REMOVING THE RESIDUE)

With all the cleansing and purging, I was going through. God moved on me to go back and forgive everyone that had ever hurt my children and me. One day, I was visiting a familiar church with Prince and I ran into the husband of the sitter that violated my daughter many years before. Since I was visiting, I was asked to say a few words. I stood and gave the usual accolades to the Pastor and so on. I explained that God was teaching me to forgive people. I did not know what I was about to do next, but I let the Lord word my mouth. I asked the husband to please stand and the Holy Ghost took it from there. I pointed my hand toward him and said that I forgave him and that I loved him. I felt an issue flow down my arm and out of the hand I was pointing towards him. I felt a peace come upon me and a dark weight was instantly lifted. I wasn't just running my mouth; I really forgave him from my heart. It was only by the power of God that this came to be. In time past, I really hated that man. Prince said he felt the power of God when I said I forgave the man; he witnessed the miraculous move of God.

I then made my calls to Tim, Doris, Victor, Maurice, Mr. and Mrs. Hurt, and Jerome. I told them that I forgave them and asked them to forgive me for holding un-forgiveness in my heart towards them. They were all unbelievably lost for words and I could feel their hearts beginning to mend. I could feel the bitterness loosening from my spirit. Now after all the years of praying for a husband I was now married to Prince, the one I dreamed of having babies with many years before. He really appreciated me as a woman of God and knew so much about the Word.

Our sex life was unbelievable. We actually felt a connection that could not be explained. It was a perfect fit and not just physically. Though his heart was very fragile, he had a gentle spirit, and since he was unable to exercise a sense of humor, it made my kidding jesters hard to express. However, he helped encourage my children to do certain chores and we all enjoyed coming together for family prayer. He would not let me do anything after getting home from work until I took a shower and changed into something more comfortable. I had never taken a shower so early in the evening before, but it only took me a couple days to get used to it. I was so used to rushing home and trying to prepare something for the kids to eat.

Prince would always have dinner cooked, or at least it was started by the time I got home. It was wonderful having the help. I felt like we would finally be functional. But just within a few weeks, he was showing his other side. You know the one that most people hide from everyone else. He seemed to be very unhappy, restless and uncomfortable within himself.

About 6 months after our marriage, he stopped going to church because he couldn't get off work. What a flash back, just like Tim did 6 months after we were married. How could this be? God confirmed our marriage. What kind of mess was this? The kids had gotten use to doing their chores and had developed a bit of respect for Prince. They could see that he was a help to me both financially and as a companion even though they noticed an inconsistency in his behavior.

Finally, he admitted that he was struggling with his addiction again. I knew he used to smoke and drink but I did not know he was also using crack. I didn't know what to do when he told me that. I had heard so many stories about crack heads; he just didn't fit the bill. I just looked to God and reminded him of his promises he made to me concerning my marriage to Prince. I did not realize how serious his struggle with the addictions would affect us all. I was determined to help him through this. God put us together for some reason.

Every 3 or 6 months Prince would have a relapse and go away for a couple of days. Usually the weekend he was paid. His checks stopped making it home and our food supply was getting low. My daughter asked, "Why was this happening?"
She thought we would not have to go without since I was married now. I didn't know how to answer her, so I said, "I thought the same thing too." I didn't explain what was going on with Prince to the kids. It was too early it would have crushed them. Especially my son, he really liked Prince and they had a wonderful relationship. He was the only man in his life that spent any positive time with him. I had to endure with Prince, God kept telling me to show him love, and I kept asking God to show me how.

We had purchased another vehicle months earlier so that we could both get to our jobs easily. But making the payment became impossible after Prince kept smoking up his paychecks. He was in and out of jobs at the drop of a hat. All I wanted was a promotion on my job and could not get one. I couldn't understand why God would continually show him favor when I was financially struggling and so emotionally confused. I actually got to a point where I was jealous of how much God would continually bless him and show him favor with all kinds of people. I was losing weight from lack of food and feeling so ashamed of all that was happening. Our tender sex life was closed down and I found myself married and still sleeping alone. My hair was coming out in patches. By this time, my children knew what was going on and was hoping God would work his miracle soon. God did not move quick enough for me.

After the prayers of my Pastor, and me anointing his shoes, toothbrush, clothes, and anything I could find of his to anoint, talking to him and learning to just shut up sometimes. Nothing was changing. It only grew worse. Even though he would always apologize and try to bring a check or two home, it didn't matter. The damage had already been done. I was letting him drive my car to get to work or where ever, but once I found out he was taking it out of town to do drugs, I took it back. I gave it to a friend that needed it more than he did. There was no catching up on some of the bills at this point.

Then one day after he had given me most of his paycheck, he left to get a hit and came back later that evening. He got up and went to church with us and I took him to work after service. When we returned home, my son noticed his game gear with all the games and case were missing. I was furious; I wanted to blow up every crack house I could find. This crack devil was not playin and I just thought about all the families that were being destroyed because of it. Why did God have me marry this fool? My life was coming along just fine before Prince came back into my life. My children did not need to be hurt and disappointed anymore. Why was I commissioned to such a union with Prince? This wasn't fair. I called Prince at work and asked him about the game gear. He acted as though he didn't even know what it was. When he finally took a chance and knocked on the door at 2:00am, I told him he could not come in. He just said okay and left with the friend that brought him home. I had heard about tough love, now I was about to experience it.

God kept telling me that he needed me to show Prince Godly love. Something he had never received before, but where were the blessings God promised me? The brother had some serious issues, I could not help him, I didn't know how to help myself, but then I would remember what God told me a couple of years before. He said to prepare for my husband and that he would need what I had. "What I had?" God wasn't talking about things, He was talking about love. All I was commissioned to do was show him love. What a charge to keep! Talking about loving one another, at this point love did not seem to matter. The more I loved him, the more he seemed to take it for granted. But it wasn't that at all, he just didn't know how to respond to it. I learned that if love has never been introduced to a person it is like foreign matter to them, like an irritant. They are afraid to trust it and it's hard for them to receive it.

The first reaction to unfamiliar things is rejection. Prince wasn't rejecting the kids or me, he was rejecting God. It was then that I understood how God wanted to use me. I knew love; it was a familiar matter to me. We all seek love and desire it more than the breath we breathe. I was yearning to be loved by my husband I craved his affection. Prince addicted to drugs and rejection and though he hated the ramifications, he still craved it. God uses us to distribute his love; he needed a willing vessel to impart it to Prince. God was showing me what love had to do with it, and that he had equipped me to impart it to Prince. Woo, lucky me, my children and I were the chosen ones; (with all pun intended).

It was almost strange to say, but I did not hate Prince, nor did I want to give up on him. I did not want him in the home if he was going to steal from us though and I had to do my best to protect the children too. All I could feel for him was love, not pity, not retribution, but love. I knew God was in this venue for sure because without him it would have been impossible. It was as if God was holding all other emotions back and only allowing love to seep through. I thanked him for the strength he had given me, for it was not of my own.

I didn't allow Prince to come back in the house. He had to seek refuge somewhere else. He eventually went to a rehab center and the children felt like their things were safe. My son was heartbroken he really loved Prince. I was still working and going to church and I had to keep smiling because it helped me to endure.

Before long, Octavia and I were blessed to gain a new member. Her name was Star. She was definitely anointed to give God the praise and lead us into worship. She joined with Octavia and me, so the spiritual attacks did not seem as bad as they had been before. I now had someone to help me fight through the oppositions. The Lord was blessing us in the services, but more than anyone I was being strengthened delivered and set free. I was very sincere every time I went forth in praise and worship. I did it from my heart. I loved praising God. I knew what he had done for me and how blessed I was to be able to stand in praise before him. It was a privilege, a benefit and an honor.

Prince was gone about three weeks now and was staying

with some of his friends. We had been communicating via phone from time to time. We went to church together and God ministered to Prince in bible class, the praise service and the morning message. One day after service, he said he needed to tell me something. I thought now what? I didn't know if I wanted to hear it or not, but he assured me it was nothing he had done recently. It was something that happened way before I ever met him. He had never shared it with anyone, but he knew he should share it with me. When he told me I was stunned, and my heart wept. I knew about the abandonment and abuse he suffered as a child but not this. I was numb and my love for him swelled. He was so thankful to God for the love he had gifted our marriage with and relieved that I didn't reject him. I asked the Lord about letting him come back home but he said not yet. Prince asked if I would fast and pray with him over the next week and I did.

After four weeks, I got a merit raise on my job. It wasn't as much as I wanted but it was more than I had. Prince lost his job. The van payment had become overbearing so I decided to do a voluntary repo. Now we had no transportation and the church van had to pick us up for church services. No one asked questions, Pastor already knew what was going on. It was so embarrassing and the kids felt so ashamed. I asked God "how high and lifted up was I to have to be so humiliated?" Though I knew I was supposed to marry Prince, I felt like the biggest fool. I wanted to run away from it all and just go to sleep until it was over, but I had no desire to backslide again. If I seemed like I was waddling in the mud with pigs again, it wasn't because I decided to lie there and die. No, not now. This time, though muddy and perplexed, you would actually witness me callously and violently fighting for my life, my value, and my inheritance. I wasn't turning my back on God this time. I now knew that he loved me more than anyone could ever think to love me.

Weeks later Prince was living back home and late in the evening I found myself wondering where he was. I didn't know what to do or say at this point. I wanted to scream and then again, maybe I wanted to cry myself to sleep. I realized I could not pick up the phone to call for help, because no one could. "Jesus is the author and finisher of our faith". (Hebrews 12:2) Only he understands. I didn't know what to say or think and even though I was full of emotion, I couldn't choose what to feel. Why was Prince doing this to us? Why was he doing it to himself? Why? Why?

I had promised the kids that I would take them to the movies, but because of the lack of finances and other problems Prince had caused, I was not able to keep my word. This was not the norm for my kids. They were used to me keeping my promises. I could not afford to promise them anything anymore. I did not want them to think I was lying intentionally. My daughter and I needed our hair attended to by a professional because it was badly damaged. We didn't have the hair products to groom or keep it healthy. I had a small bald patch on the back of my head. Thank God, my hair was long enough to cover the bald spot. Asking for help was a joke. No one wanted to help you if you "got a man" to take care of you. In some cases, I couldn't get help because the man I was married to was not respected. Because of the actions or characteristics of your spouse, I learned that people will shun you. What was I being punished for? Why so much hurt, embarrassment and shame? I had been faithful to Prince. In the four years we had been married I wasn't doing drugs; I lived holy and did all I could to stay above water. I felt ugly and unattractive at times. I would think about the promises God spoke to me, but some days I felt so alone.

However, I noticed God had not told me to keep showing Prince love anymore. I still loved him, and treated him the same, but the season had changed. God told me to refrain from embracing. He actually spoke those words to my spirit. You will find in the book of Ecclesiastes that it speaks of the different seasons and time. Ecclesiasts 3:5 says, "...a time to embrace, and a time to refrain from embracing" I felt such a calm in my spirit. I knew my commission to help Prince was almost complete.

Two months later Prince was gone for good. He obviously chose the crack over us. Almost three years after marrying him, I was ready to let go. Yet my spiritual man had changed. I felt stronger and greatly purged. I was finding out who I really was and that God actually had an eternal purpose for me. It was as if he used the whole trial to refine Prince, the children and I to reach a level in him that we never imagined. My heart bled for anyone who needed deliverance. The gift of discernment burst free and the gift of prophecy began to flow. I understood what God meant about being a living sacrifice. (Read Romans 12:1). I didn't have to physically die for Prince, but my mindset had to be changed and my emotions had to succumb to the will of God. I learned to leave people's opinions where they belong, to themselves.

Another year had passed and as far as the law of the land, Prince had physically abandoned us. My constant prayer was for God to please help me regroup. My silent scream was full of fear. Faith was not present when the collectors kept calling. They wouldn't believe me when I told them that Prince was not there. In the four years we had been married Prince was only home a total of one year and that was not twelve months straight.

One day I was sitting in church and the praise was going forth in an unusual manner. We were all at our seats and I was praising and worshipping God in spite of all that had happened. Then the Holy Spirit (God) spoke to me and said, "I Release you". I continued to worship him afraid to believe what I just heard. Then I heard the spirit of God say, "You have been faithful through trials and temptations, I release you". I began to weep uncontrollably. The Pastor came over to me and just held me and ministered to me in tongues. I began to think, could God do that? Can he actually release me? Well, of course. He's God!!! He can do whatever he chooses, he is sovereign. I just knew no one would believe me, but I knew what I heard. I was free, no longer chained to Prince and the reproach he brought upon my children and me. I felt like the world was lifted off my shoulders.

The aftermath left me disappointed and frustrated, even though I somewhat understood why God asked me to marry Prince. I wondered why He put us together if we were going to be apart. My minuscule mind couldn't begin to dilute this purpose or cause and then the Lord said, "Did not I make Eve for Adam?" ~Hmm, I'll let you chew on that one yourself. ~

God's Holy Spirit continued to call me into communion, but I ignored his plea. My attitude was carnal and I just wanted to lay low like everyone else. It seemed easier that way. I did not want to pray because I was afraid of what God was going to tell me to do next. I found that with every promise he gave me, I would have to fight to possess it. The battles were too strenuous for me and I just wanted to rest. I could not believe

God expected so much from me. I felt like everything was so unfair and I didn't want to talk to him anymore. It was too frightening. But the Holy Spirit continued to beckon me. Finally, he told me to just write him a letter. I didn't want to write the letter either. I had nothing to say. Nevertheless, the tenderness of his beckoning forced me to pick up a pen and write. While I pondered about all that I went through, I could not believe how the words began to flow out as if they were in competition with the tears that accompanied them. This is what I wrote:

'I long to be with you, to hear soft words that put my mind to ease. Your embrace once felt now only lingers as a memory. Ever since you told me, divine instruction, the perfect plan. The fear that tried to embrace me, melted away as I submitted to your desire. I closed my eyes as I said yes and fell back into your arms. You held me, but for a little while, then released me to go forward. I moved by your command with hope right beside me, and I saw your vision, perfect and true. But along the way the plan, your instructions became painful to watch and at times, hard to endure. When I called you, you would listen, only to tell me to hold on, go on with the plan, but the comfort I sought, the words I once heard, full of life and glorious things, now seemed dead to my ear. I felt alone and confused, wondering if what we had was really real. I stopped calling you; your loyalty seemed far gone, non-existing. My life, my breath, my destiny, my purpose all rested upon you. I miss talking to you and the secrets you would share but I fight a continual battle of trusting, hoping again. I know I can't possibly understand the reason, the purpose, the why. At least not it all, but I know that the relationship we once had gave me joy, peace and the feeling of completeness. I long for you more

than the breath I breathe, my best friend, my confidant. Please call me and speak those words of serenity, heal my hurts and cast out all the confusion. I miss our time, our talks our thing. Forgive me for not trusting you through all that has happened, for leaning to my own understanding which is none. Take me back, please hold me again, stroke my brow and tell me again of your love for me. I need you, I miss you, I love you. Touch me and I will know I will remember the realness I once felt. Hear my heart see my tears, remind me that I'm special to you and that no one else is like me. Let me know you will always be in my corner as long as I'm in yours. Call me anytime; I'll be open to receive...'

I could not believe the relief I felt, I ended up praying anyway. I just had to chuckle. God got me again. I also felt an empowerment from the whole experience and found that God was going to talk to me in spite of myself.

Even though I felt constrained to the marriage, I longed to be free. So when I talked to Prince, I told him I wanted a divorce and though he understood he did not want the divorce. I had kept my wedding vows and knew I had done all I could do as his wife. Just like Tim, Prince didn't understand that marriage is a covenant, not a contract; and they both fell short of their part long before God released me.

Chapter 18

THE PEARL

Our Church went through a season of wonderful praise services and then the enemy came with new tactics. I would begin singing a song and the words would just evaporate out of my mind. I would end up standing there like some idiot that just couldn't seem to get it together. My memory was under attack and I didn't want anyone to know. It was affecting my performance at work and even conversations I would have with people. I did not want to tell anyone because I thought it was my problem. I never wanted to make it seem like I was just trying to make excuses or to give anyone a reason to call me crazy.

I sang when I was sick and when I felt like God was nowhere to be found. I praised him when my children and I were hungry and did not know how I was going to pay the rent. I praised him when the Congregation didn't seem like they wanted to give God the glory. Nevertheless, he had done too much for me. I knew my redeemer lived and I believed that leading his people in praise was the least I could do for him. Whether he moved in my life ever again, I owed him praise. I was created to praise him at all times.

One day after service, the Lord told me to shake the only $10 I had in the hand of a young man that attended the church.

I thought but God, this is all I have to buy the kids and me something to eat. But the Holy Ghost insisted that I give it, so I did. I felt sort of foolish but hoped God would move for us in some way. Two days later, on a Monday afternoon, someone shook a $2000.00 check in my hand. That's right, $2000.00. God had blown my mind this time. I found out that he doesn't add to your sacrificial seeds, he multiplies. He had taken my faith to another level for sure.

I asked God how I could ever forgive myself for the abortion I committed and he told me to tell the baby I was sorry. I didn't know how that was possible, but then I realized our spirit never dies. My baby was with him and he was willing to let me talk to it. He said, "Just tell her you're sorry". Her? Tell her? It was a girl. I always wondered now I knew. I thought this was strange but I closed my eyes and began to cry. I began to tell my baby I was sorry and the Lord let me see her. She looked to be about two years old and she was a precious medium brown tone. Her coarse, coal black hair was parted down the middle and each side was pulled together creating a soft afro puff. I could not see her eyes but she had strong cheek bones covered with round meaty flesh, just like Maurice's and her teeth were small but brilliantly white. I told her I was sorry and that I really did love her. She smiled with a joyful hop and said, "That's okay mommy". I wept uncontrollably. She called me mommy! That day, I felt so much heaviness released from my being. I instantly knew what her name was; it was like a sparkling diamond glistening throughout her entire soul. Grace is her name. God loved me enough to allow me the privilege of seeing her. He granted me peace of mind. Who wouldn't serve a God like him?

During this period, I talked to Jerome off and on via

telephone and sometimes we would meet for lunch. God was miraculously changing his mindset and heart from harboring so much bitterness and hurt. The Lord had connected him to a wonderful church family and his Pastor was a great mentor in teaching him about being a man of God. He would call me to ask questions about the Lord or commend me for always being there for him as a sister and friend. He began to learn how to relate to people in a healthy manner and he became very faithful to his church. God began to bless his finances and he began getting awards at his job. He started paying tithes and the Lord just opened up all kinds of doors for him. The Lord was teaching him how to see women as human beings and not objects. Jerome learned that his ability to master mind and conjure up ways of survival were not from his own power or wit, but that God was his source of strength, skill and survival. We have remained friends over the years and God has blessed him to become debt free. My prayers of over 10 years ago had been answered. Hallelujah, God saved Jerome!

Jerome says if it were not for his Pastor, and me he would have never found the Lord to be such a good and gracious God. Jerome's testimony inspired me not to give up on anyone that is seeking truth. God can do anything if we only believe. Jerome has since been a blessing to my children and me, by buying us food or making sure any house repairs were taken care of. His heart went out to us during my difficult marriage. He actually became a friend.

Chapter 19

ৡৡৡ

THE PRESENTATION
(RECEIVING THE CALL)

After almost 8 years of leading in praise and worship, I finally regained my singing ability. I thank God for Octavia and Star. They really pushed me to go forth and give God the glory. Octavia would make me sing out and took me back to my alto/contralto mode. When I first started singing with her, I was always trying to sing too low, because my spirit was low. It almost took a decade for reconciliation to place me back in unity with my Lord and Savior.

I recall one day the Holy Ghost spoke to me and requested me to go to work with my hair neatly combed back and not to worry about curling it. It was my daily ritual to curl my hair. I did not believe I had enough beauty of my own to not have my hair together. Moreover, if my hair was not presentable, I would definitely pass the nice appearance task by wearing makeup. Deborah and I always thought we were bearable to look at, but we did not think we were pretty or anything close to it. Therefore, I thought at this point what did I have to lose. Besides, I have had bad hair days many times before. So as I thought about applying my makeup the Lord said no. For the whole week, he instructed me to just comb my hair back and leave the makeup alone. The Holy Spirit inspired me to walk with my head up as if my hair was at its best, as if I had no flaws. Talk about feeling naked before everyone.

Woo, my first day was a surprising experience. As I walked around smiling with my head up high, no one made a smart remark. No one shunned me or laughed at my appearance. Since I took on the attitude of beauty, no one argued the matter. When the week ended, I found an inward peace I never experienced before. Though I never thought I was unattractive, I never thought I was beautiful. That weekend I was at a stoplight and I felt like the person in the car to my left was staring at me. The car seemed to be from the 70's and needed a serious paint job. I glanced out of the corner of my eye and there was a young white man of large bone structure. He was playing some sort of booming music as he sat unsettled in his seat. He had bleached blonde hair and appeared to be unlearned in some way. He continued gazing at me in an unusual manner. So I felt to look at him to see what was up. I just knew he was going to say something derogatory or call me out of my name. When I looked at him eye to eye, he opened his mouth and said "You ugly!"

I immediately knew who he was. The devil sent one of his imps to challenge me. I just smiled and began to chuckle. The light turned green and while he was still looking at me, he slowly sped away. It seemed as though everything was in slow motion. As I pulled into the gas station I just laughed and began saying; "I am not ugly, praise God, I am not ugly." If someone had said that to me just a few days before I would have accepted it. But I now knew that God had delivered me from that lie. I didn't know I had such a low self-esteem. The bible says, "I was fearfully and wonderfully made" (Psalm 139:14). God was making me whole by renewing my mind.

After so many ups and downs, God definitely used the devil to help shape and refine me. I came out completely restored and called to serve as a minister and teacher of the Gospel.

The Lord blessed me to get a new job at a new company with an increase in pay. The kids and I got a new car and moved into our first house. The financial struggles were slowly easing up and my children were back to trusting my promises again.

Pastor Ruth had pulled me back on track with her fasting and prayers. My purpose was redefined and I began to recognize the road my steps were being ordained to walk. I began to wean myself from people that were not about Godly living. I had to sanctify myself from them. The bible says to "come out from them and be separate, says the Lord" (II Cor 6:17 NIV). I no longer felt comfortable around everyone. My desires had changed. My friend Deana reconciled with God and left her man of over 10 years. I was so happy she and her baby girl were safe now. My daughter was a continual inspiration for me to keep the praises going up. She was my backbone over the years and I really thank God for her in my life. My son began to display his gift as a musician and now gives all glory and honor to God. The soberness of mind I thought I possessed was incomplete. Soberness does not apply to the physical consumption but it applies to our spiritual minds as well. In the Amplified version of the Holy bible, 1Peter 4:7-10 says, "...therefore be clear minded and self-controlled so that you can pray. Above all, love each other deeply, because love covers over a multitude of sins. Offer hospitality to one another without grumbling. Each one should use whatever gift he has received to serve others, faithfully administering God's grace in its various forms".

My sexual desires did not die, but as time went on the Lord taught me how to discipline myself. I became a better gate keeper in protecting my ear, eye, nose, and mouth gates. I began to be more conscious of who and what I listened to (i.e. music), more selective on what I viewed on television, stayed away from luring smells (i.e. men's cologne), stopped flirting so much, and became more knowledgeable of foods that may cause an aphrodisiacal reaction. I learned to find comfort in God's Word, in prayer and in His presence.

I should have never displaced my value but the Holy Spirit reminded me of whom I was in the Lord. I had cast my pearly virtue among the pigs and almost lost my place in the eternal kingdom. But because of God's grace and mercy and definitely his Word and love, he gave me a second chance. He really did take me out of the miry clay and place my feet on a rock to stay. While reading the bible, in the book of Haggai, I learned that if I build his house he will without doubt bless mine.

My fellow sisters and brothers, please never devalue the purpose God has placed in you. No matter what may come our way, we were all created and predestined by him. As jewels or strands of pearls, we must be willing to build his Kingdom with the tools he has equipped us with. He has given us all talent, time and testimonies. The beautiful pearl has been cleansed; purged and polished. I am willing to build his Kingdom with the tools he has equipped me with. All the word I studied as a child was good for laying a foundation. However, reading about Jesus cannot compare to the joy of knowing him. You can have master degrees upon masters, but if you never develop a covenant relationship with God, the letter cannot be as effective in your life.

I shared a message with my church family once. It was entitled "Loosed". It was about Paul and Silas praying, and singing praises while bound in prison, (Read Acts 16:16-40). It really reflects the position I was in while leading praise and worship during my "loosing stage". In the 35th verse, it speaks of what happened in the daylight, morning had come. The devil was fully exposed and justification prevailed. I was able to see clearly now and my identity was reclaimed. The Holy Ghost reminded me of whose I was and all that God said I am. Here are just a few things that I began to declare:

<u>I am</u>

The righteousness of God
Redeemed by his blood
A chosen people
Healed by his stripes
Anointed and appointed
Fearfully and wonderfully made
Dead to sin and risen in Christ
The apple of God's eye
No longer cursed but blessed
Justified freely by his grace
Filled with his spirit
Full of power and authority over all devils
Ordained to praise
More than a conqueror
The light and the salt of the world
Given beauty for ashes
The house that manifest the presence of God
The bride of God
A royal priest hood
A pearl of great value

As it is written in Matthew 13:44-46 (NIV), "the kingdom of heaven is like treasure hidden in a field. When a man found it, he hid it again, and then in his joy went and sold all he had and bought that field. Again, the kingdom of heaven is like a merchant looking for fine pearls. When he found one of great value, he went away and sold everything he had and bought it". God gave his only begotten son, because we are valuable to him. The blood of Jesus paid the price and redeemed us back from all iniquity. That virtuous woman I mentioned at the beginning of this book is back. Even so, I am much more mature and have come to understand the subject by my life experiences. I found out that my value really is far above rubies.

God had to restore my hope in meeting a Godly man on this planet and now that my faith has been restored, I definitely know I will be a virtuous wife again. God told me I had been looking for the Adam before the fall, the one without sin. He said that that Adam no longer exists. Instead there are redeemed Adams that have been refined and redeemed after the fall and that He will bless me with one of them. That man of valor will know how to maintain my worth and will afford the cost of my upkeep.

I have identified the enemy for who he really is, a spirit mostly found in a hurting and confused human form. My plan to proceed with teaching and preaching to all that seek their value, their purpose and their God, has been launched by revealing my mistakes to you. Though embarrassing in one aspect, it has been a level of cleansing from my past in another. I have confessed with the intention of exposing the devil so that my messes can be a revealing message to you. Jesus said, "The thief comes only in order to steal and kill and destroy. I came that they may have and enjoy life, and have it in abundance (to the full, till it overflows)" John 10:10 AMP.

There is a standard God is requiring of His people and especially His leaders. Holiness must be exemplified in the lives of those God has called; so they can become the chosen. Then the flock will no longer be fearful or scattered; the good shepherds will rise and the people will be blessed.
(Read Jeremiah 23:1-4)

I want everyone to be able to walk in liberty, having life more abundantly as God intended. Practice what Paul wrote in Romans 12:2. "Do not be conformed to this world, but be transformed by the renewal of your mind, so that you may prove what is the good and acceptable and perfect will of God".

Always remember that there has never been and will never be unity among virtuous souls and foul spirits; or as I put it, Pearls & Pigs.

THE NEW BEGINNING

www.ingramcontent.com/pod-product-compliance
Lightning Source LLC
Chambersburg PA
CBHW051838040426
42447CB00006B/590